Newly Single Woman

The Guidebook to be Happy, Healthy, and Safe

Jessica –
I wish you
a life of Health,
Happiness, Safety,
and Safety!
live in possibility!

Joy –
Caitlan

ISBN: 978-0-6921704-3-4 paperback

Printed in the United States of America
First Printing, 2018

This book is dedicated to my daughters.
I pray you will always be
Happy, Healthy, and Safe.

You inspire and motivate me to be the best woman
I can be. Thank you for all the wonderful years;
past, present, and future, sharing, learning, and
overcoming life challenges together.

I love you with my whole heart,
now and forever.

And also to my parents who raised me to think
positive and to set and reach my goals. Thank you.
I love you both.

To my fabulous lifelong friends: Kat, Suzanne,
Noelle, Robin, and Keith. Thank you for being
there with me through so much and always
making me feel so loved; for cheering me on
through the good times, and picking me up
through the tough times. I love you all.

I am incredibly blessed to have
all of these people in my life.

XO

Newly Single Woman

The Guidebook to be Happy, Healthy, and Safe

By Joy Casillas

INTRODUCTION

Since you are reading this book, I know you are a single woman trying to live your life with power and positivity. You are not used to being single and are looking for the best ways to deal with everything from fluctuating emotions to the numerous tasks and new experiences now coming into view. I know all of this can feel overwhelming at times. I know, because I have been there too. I have been a single mother of my two beautiful, now teenage daughters for 10 years. I was with their father for 20 years (starting my senior year of high school) and we divorced when my girls were just 5 and 6 years old.

I have spent years studying the patterns of women as they emerge from their relationships and live the single life. Most women go through an initial phase of pulling inward. The rapidly changing emotions that come up at this time can be so intense that just dealing with them as you get through each day becomes a challenging priority. If you have children, you naturally want to ensure their happiness, health, and safety as you work hard getting them and yourself through this process of change.

Once you have worked through your emotions and get used to the new logistics of daily life, you begin to think about how you want to live big, try new things, go new places, meet new people, create new relationships, deepen friendships, and maybe even find new love. This can be exciting and invigorating, but it also can bring up new questions, frustrations, and fears. Things may differ greatly from when you were single before and you may not know where to turn to get the answers you seek.

That is why I wrote this book. The topics here are all important to living an empowered life and to be happy, healthy, and safe as you manage your state of mind, health, beauty, finances, estate, career, home, car, relationships, safety and more. So, whatever you are feeling right now, this book will help guide you through those feelings with the knowledge you need to feel powerful and confident to live a life you love. The format is meant to be an easy-to-read guidebook on topics relevant to a Newly Single Woman, where you can flip to any section you want and read it (or re-read it) whenever you need it.

The sections are purposefully brief, presenting you with core concepts and information quickly so you do not have to wait to find large chunks of quiet time to get through long chapters or to research the many topics online. Feel free to bookmark pages and highlight information for easy reference later. You can also read the book from cover to cover - the point is to use this book your way, to bring you and your life the most value.

My intent is to:

- Provide insights and information to minimize anxiety or overwhelm you may be feeling.

- Help to define your life vision and develop plans to create your dream life.

- Deliver resources and ideas to expand your perspectives and tools to live with powerfully.

- Knowledge on topics which are critical to living your dream life.

- Empower you to be happy, healthy and safe as you build this new chapter of your life.

There are many questions and thought activities presented throughout this book to help you connect with the concepts.

I have included blank pages at the end of each section and at the back of the book for you to make notes and lists for yourself. As thoughts come up at any point in your reading, I suggest you take a moment to make a note to yourself and add the page number that inspired the note so you can reference it later.

I wish all good things to flow to you, and for you to grab them and build on them to create a life you love! May you embark on many new experiences that re-ignite and enliven your mind, body, and spirit!

"Go confidently in the direction of your dreams.
Live the life you have imagined."
– Henry David Thoreau

Warmly,

Joy Casillas

"Every beginning comes from some other beginning's end." ~Seneca	"It's never too late to be who you might have been." ~George Elliott	"Rock bottom became the solid foundation on which I rebuilt my life." ~JK Rowlings
"To be yourself in a world that is constantly trying to make you something else is the greatest accomplishment." ~Ralph Waldo Emerson	"The talent for being happy is appreciating and liking what you have, instead of what you don't have." ~Woody Allen	"The secret of change is to focus all of your energy, not on fighting the old, but on building the new." ~Socrates
"Have the courage to follow your heart and intuition. They somehow know what you truly want to become." ~Steve Jobs	"Life is very interesting. In the end, some of your greatest pains become your greatest strengths." ~Drew Barrymore	"No matter how your heart is grieving, if you can keep on believing, the dreams that you wish will come true." ~Cinderella
"Just when the caterpillar thought the world was over, it became a butterfly." ~Proverb	"What lies behind you and what lies in front of you, pales in comparison to what lies inside of you." ~Ralph Waldo Emerson	"What makes you different or weird – that is your strength." ~Meryl Streep

Table of Contents

Be Happy.

"Happy girls are the prettiest." ~Audrey Hepburn	"If you want to live a happy life, tie it to a goal. Not to people or things." ~Albert Einstein	"Think of all the beauty still left around you and be happy." ~Anne Frank
"Happiness is not a goal. It's a by-product of a life well lived." ~Eleanor Roosevelt	"Most folks are as happy as they make up their minds to be." ~Abraham Lincoln	"The surest way to be happy is to seek happiness for others" ~Martin Luther King
Happiness is the secret to all beauty. There is no beauty without happiness." ~Christian Dior	"Happiness is when what you think, what you say, and what you do are in harmony." ~Mahatma Gandhi	"Happiness is not something ready-made. It comes from your own actions." ~ Dalai Lama XIV
"It is the ultimate luxury to combine passion and contribution. It is also a very clear path to happiness." ~Sheryl Sandberg	"If you have good thoughts they will shine out of your face like sunbeams and you will always look lovely." Roald Dahl	"I think happiness is what makes you pretty. Period. Happy people are beautiful. They become like a mirror and they reflect that happiness." ~Drew Barrymore

HAPPINESS

This section is written to help you understand and optimize every lever you have to create, increase and manage your own happiness each day. You will learn about how the way you think impacts your happiness level, the science of how happiness flows, and the key components to create a life you love.

Mindsets

Do you know the story of the honeybee? Based on all the laws of physics, for the last seventy years, scientists had agreed that the honeybee physically could not fly. And yet they do every day, and have for hundreds of years! Studying the bee structure shows that their wings are too small to support the size and weight of their own body. Yet, they fly. Really, this was a mystery of physics for decades.

Finally, when scientists had the right technology they figured out what was actually happening. They filmed the flight of the honeybee and saw that to compensate for the smaller wings the bees beat their wings super-fast, like 230 beats per minute! Not only that but the beat of the wings creates a "mini-hurricane" around the bee allowing them to lift and fly more efficiently.

I love this story because it demonstrates there are many ways to achieve our goals. Don't allow yourself to focus on your perceived limitations. Too often we focus on our beliefs that we have limits and cannot do what we want to do. The truth is that the less we focus on our perceived limitations, and focus more on solutions and actions, the more the world will open up to us and enable us to achieve greater than we have ever imagined.

Since your thoughts play such an important role in your ability to create and live a life you love, seriously consider your mindsets and how they will affect the possibilities you allow yourself to cultivate.

Growth vs. Fixed Mindsets

The difference between a growth and fixed mindset is your belief that you will continue to grow and change throughout your life vs. the belief that the person you are today, or the way situations are today, are the way they will remain forever.

When you are in a growth mindset you know that you can, and will, learn new things all throughout your life and that every new thing learned will add a little piece more to your being. You can look at life with a sense of excited expectation for what may present itself.

Every day presents new fascinating opportunities to see, do, feel, and learn something new! Even when times are hard, when you have a growth mindset, you look for the lessons to be learned and/or to find fascination in something.

The opposite of this is a fixed mindset where you maintain a sense of cynicism or boredom with life. The belief that nothing will change and that you are doomed to live every day of your life the same. Logically we can conceive this is not even possible. Even if you lived exactly the same way every day, things around you will change. To live we must grow. We can embrace and enjoy and facilitate our growth, or we can eventually be forced into change by time and the universe.

Think about what have you learned throughout your life. Have you learned how to walk? How to talk?
How to read and write? Have you learned to drive a car, or cook a meal? Do you know how to play a musical instrument or a sport? Do you know how to send an email, search the internet, and use your cell phone?
At some point in your life you did not know these things and through experience and practice you learned and changed and grew. That process of growth never stops. At any point in your life, you can learn and change.

Activity: *Now you have been reminded of many of the awesome things you have learned and achieved in your life, what can you think of that you want to learn next?*

As you read through this book, this question may come up often. Explore in your mind what intrigues and fascinates you. What would you be interested in exploring and learning further now? As you do this you will develop and strengthen your growth mindset.

Abundance vs. Scarcity

Similar to the growth mindset, the abundance belief is that there is always an abundance of good things in life for everyone. Whether that is money, love, friendship, food, opportunity, ideas, or even quality single men. The belief holds that if you expect that you will always have an abundance of all good things, that life will return an abundance of all good things to you.

The scarcity mindset fools you into thinking there is a limited number of things in the universe. If you focus on your lack of anything then life will produce the lack you are creating. You will see lack everywhere to validate your assumption. The belief that there is not enough can cause you to feel frustrated, sad, hopeless, and jealous of others, thinking there is no more for you to have. However, if you focus your mind on abundance and believe that there is more than enough for everyone, you will create thoughts that lead you to solutions that when acted upon brings whatever you need to you to fulfill your dreams.

I know you have probably experienced this phenomenon already in your own life. When you focus on creating a solution to a challenge you are facing, thoughts present new ideas and they each build on one another to get you to the solution(s) needed. One way to energize your process is to involve others. The power of combining minds to brainstorm ideas reaps massive rewards since each person involved can bring in new perspectives and knowledge from their unique experiences. There is an abundance of ideas in the universe too, so allow yourself the time and space to ponder and you will be amazed at what comes up for you.

Activity: Think of one thing in your life you would like more of. Money is a good example since that is the first thing many people will say. So, on a piece of paper write at the top "Money consistently flows to me from many sources." Then list underneath all the ways money could show up for you. You can even brainstorm with a friend. Think of ways you can bring value to others. List at least ten to twenty ideas. Even if your ideas seem silly at first, they may grow on you and lead you to new opportunities to realize all the abundance meant for you.

As an example, here is how this list played out for me. (You may see a few things on here that I have since completed.)

Money consistently flows to me from many sources.

- *I can ask for a raise at my job*
- *I can get a new job*
- *I can get a second job*
- *I can sell items I no longer need*
- *I can take out a loan*
- *I can book more life coach clients*
- *I can speak at events*
- *I can start an online business*
- *I can write and publish a book*
- *I can start a bakery business on a food truck*
- *I can get a roommate*
- *I can babysit*
- *I can recycle*

Power vs. Victim

Power and empowerment are largely what this book is about. I have witnessed many women (myself included) feel sorrow, frustration, and anger after a long relationship ends. This is normal after a loss. I feel so deeply for women going through this and I am sending out my vibes of support to you as you read this book.

If you sit in these emotions for too long your thoughts can turn to the "why me" or "I didn't deserve this" or "it is all their fault" type of thinking. That is the victim mentality and it is very DIS-empowering. It can grab ahold of you and make you feel worse as you continue to spin on the same thoughts over and over. When you think like this, you allow yourself to believe that you don't control what happens in your life and you can forget that you have power in the choices you make.

Instead, after allowing yourself some time to acknowledge the sadness or anger you have felt, the most powerful thing you can do is focus on the choices in your life now. Some choices we face may be difficult or even unwanted but you do have a choice. Even if you choose not to decide, you still have made a choice. You have a choice in what you say each day (to yourself and to others), how you respond to people/things, the attitudes and perspectives you keep, how you spend your free time, etc.

It is powerful to establish new mindsets. It is powerful to take on growth and abundance and to drive change in your life. You have taken powerful action in reading this book. Acknowledging there are areas you feel overwhelmed or uncertain and finding resources to help you gain knowledge to reduce these feelings is awesome power. You are not sitting, waiting, and wishing. You have taken action and that creates power within you. The more action you take the more momentum you will drive in your life to create the life you dream of. As you read through this book you will undoubtedly find information on topics that make you think, "I want to do that," or "I want to try that." When those thoughts come up be sure to make note of them, then walk yourself through the steps to do, try, and/or complete it. You will see that as you push yourself through each action that your power and confidence will grow and that your feelings of overwhelm and uncertainty will be reduced!

Gratitude vs. Want

Have you read and/or heard a lot of talk about gratitude and how it can change your life for the better? There is a reason that just about every person that writes or speaks about happiness lists gratitude as a critical component in sustaining a happy, satisfied life. The mindset of feeling gratitude is so pivotal because, to feel grateful, you first must have acknowledged something that you are grateful for. By doing that you are identifying positive things in your life you already have vs. all the things you may want.

It is easy to look around you and see many things you may want. The more you think about what you want, the less you see the good in what you already possess. You will become more stressed and less happy. Not only that, but the stress can take a toll on your body and you can feel more run down, get sick more often, and act irritable toward yourself and others.

When you focus on the good you have in your life, you will become a happier person. Being more grateful and happier also makes you more likable to others that want to be around your positive energy so you can create more positive relationships. Thoughts of gratitude also reduce the time and energy we spend thinking stressful thoughts and so we are clearer minded and able to make better decisions and be more productive. Studies have shown that feelings of gratitude can even decrease pain, allow for better sleep, produce more energy and optimism and therefore create a healthier, happier person overall.

There are so many ways to infuse your life with gratitude. Many people find it powerful to include gratitude in their morning and/or bedtime routines each day. When you wake up or before you go to bed, think about the things you are grateful for. Say them out loud if you can because hearing your own voice will reinforce your feelings making them deeper and richer within your heart. You can start a daily gratitude journal that you write in each day and/or even carry a gratitude stone (or any item significant to you) in your purse or pocket that reminds you each time you touch it to be thankful in that moment for something in your life. Putting a quote about gratitude on your phone lock screen or computer screen saver can also be a great way to remind yourself you have so much to be thankful for. Here are a few ways I include gratitude in my life each day:

- I "send up thank yous" many times throughout my day. Whenever something happens that I feel thankful for, I say thank you out loud. It can be loud or just a whisper but I like the way it feels to say it and hear it instead of just think it. I also like that this behavior can be observed by others nearby which can serve as a reminder to them to be grateful. I do this little ritual when the obvious good things happen in my life but I find it especially compelling when I recognize my gratitude for the avoidance of "bad" things. For example, instead of being angry at another driver for almost hitting my car and creating a car accident, I say "thank you" that the accident was avoided and continue on my way feeling better than if I stayed angry and stressed about something that almost happened.

- My mother taught me that when I am scared or can't sleep that instead of counting sheep, I can count my blessings. This not only helps re-direct and calm the mind but also generates happy grateful feelings that can help you sleep more peacefully.

- When I catch myself complaining about something, I remind myself how grateful I am to have that "thing" to complain about! If I complain about having to taxi my children all over, I think how grateful I am to have them to taxi around; when I complain about having to maintain my car or home I think how grateful I am to have them; when I complain about having to work out, I think how grateful I am to be able to move my body, etc.

The Four Mindsets

As I was finishing this mindset section, I realized that I would like to include an example of how all four mindsets can play together to create life-changing concepts and experiences. I thought about this for a while and then decided I would have to come back to this piece once I had a good example to include. This went on for many days, all the while I would write other sections of the book thinking hmmm…what would be a good example of all mindsets working powerfully together? Then it hit me. So, let me tell you about my life just before I sat down to write this book.

As you may already know, I had been a single mom for about ten years before I ever wrote a word of this book. Although I have always thought of myself as a strong example of the expression of the Growth, Abundance, Power, and Gratitude mindsets, I reached a point where my convictions were greatly tested. In September 2015 I lost a boss and friend I loved and respected immensely unexpectedly when he passed away after surgery. Then my dog, which had been with me for nineteen years, also died a month later, and in February 2016, I went through a breakup of a serious romantic relationship. This breakup was tough on me emotionally, mentally, physically, and financially. This left me in a very dark place and it seemed to linger. Even the counseling sessions I went to seemed redundant. It was especially challenging to deal with my own pain because my daughters were also saddened and disheartened by losing our dog and the end of the relationship. I knew we had to get back to a calm and happy place. And I knew it had to start with me. (Power mindset)

I got back out hiking more so I could get more time outside and exercise my body. I also knew I had to find a passion, something I could invest time into and share with my daughters and stop dwelling on my pain. After much thought, I decided that 2016 would be the "Year of Italy." I told my daughters and friends that I would take Italian language classes; learn to cook Italian homemade pasta and to visit many of the Italian restaurants in our local area. We often talked about how fun it would be to go to Italy together. (Growth and abundance mindsets)

I also started my first business at this time (growth mindset). The tide was starting to slowly change and things felt lighter and happier. Then, in September, as I was out for a quick hike one Sunday morning, I snapped my ACL and tore the Meniscus in my right knee. I was down and out and had to call 911 to send the fireman to carry me out and take me to a hospital. I was on crutches for four weeks and then had surgery and was on crutches for six more weeks. I was feeling so grateful that it was just my knee and a temporary injury that could be healed with surgery and time. (Gratitude mindset)

Now it was December and I realized my business had not taken off and I had not been profitable. I had put time, effort, and money into my business and had almost nothing to show for it. I was frustrated, embarrassed, and saddened with these results. I kept looking for an advantage in the situation (Power mindset) and I saw there could be a financial benefit in disguise. (Abundance mindset)

In January, I spoke with my tax accountant about my failing business endeavor over the last half of 2016. He

explained that my business expenses were valid expenses and that many were deductible from my income tax. By having the additional business deductions, I got an increase in my tax return which I turned into a trip to Italy for me and my daughters!
(Power and abundance mindsets)

This was the dream of my life to take my daughters to Europe! Since I knew nothing about how to travel through Europe, I spent many weeks planning the trip and booking all the hotels, travel, and tours for the sites we wanted to see. (Growth mindset)

A month before we were scheduled to go, my youngest daughter was playing defense in her school's varsity lacrosse game and snapped her ACL and meniscus in her right knee... almost six months to the day after my surgery for the same injury! This was a devastating blow to her (and all of us) since she was only halfway through her freshman lacrosse season and could play none of the remaining games. The orthopedic surgeon cleared her to still make the trip to Europe if she wore a big knee brace and we scheduled her surgery for two days after we returned. She was determined to go and I was determined to make it as easy as possible for her.
(Power mindset)

I rescheduled our travels and changed sight-seeing tours to minimize walking and rushing so we could go at her pace, all the while being so grateful that things were not worse and that we could all still go.
(Power and gratitude mindsets)

The trip was fantastic! It was all we had dreamed of and I was so proud how we all pulled together to make it come true. When we returned home we went directly into surgery and recovery mode for my daughter thinking how grateful we were that we had completed the trip. (Gratitude mindset)

There were many intense moments throughout the process of her continued recovery. At the time of this writing, it has been seven months since her surgery. She is now a sophomore and is starting lacrosse practice next week as a varsity player again. I am so happy for her! (Gratitude mindset)

During all this, it was always the shifting of my mindset that enabled me to gain control of my life again and regain my peace and happiness. By thinking in terms of growth, abundance, power, and gratitude, I saw the positives and opportunities that were there and to create the outcomes I wanted.

Had I stayed in the fixed, lack, victim, or want mindsets, I would have missed the benefits that were given to me. I could have become very angry at life and cynical had I fallen into the trap of playing the victim instead of looking for solutions or the positive outcomes I could create.

Vision Boards

A vision board is a fun way to visualize your goals. The concept of the vision board is to find images you like that reflect what you want to have, do, or be. You can also include quotes, sayings, or words to help pull it all together. I have also seen boards with only images or only words. It really depends on you. Remember that to get continued benefit out of the board after you complete it, you will want to post it somewhere where you can see it daily – in your bathroom, at a desk, by a doorway, by your bed or in the kitchen. Put your positive energy into it and imagine what it will feel like when you accomplish your goals!

Vision boards are fun to create with others also. I have done vision boarding with my daughters and their friends for years. I have also had vision board making parties with my friends where we sat, worked on our boards, drank wine and talked about our goals and visions. This created excitement for the whole group. You can do these at any time of year. There are many ways to make a vision board. I have listed a few different strategies below that you can review to see what works best for you.

Traditional Vision Boards

To make a traditional vision board, you will need a piece of poster board or cardstock that you can use as a base. (I like to use a 9x12 or 11x14 piece of poster board). You will also need various magazines that contain articles on topics related to your goals. For example, if you have business goals, Glamour may not be the right magazine for you. If you want to travel, make sure you have images of where you want to travel. You can also print images from the internet.

Scissors will be needed to clip out your images, words, sayings, and glue sticks for gluing the clippings to your board.

Digital to Print Vision Boards

Similar to the traditional boards but instead of clipping out magazine images, you can search online for specific images, quotes, words for what you want and drop them into a Word or PowerPoint document.

Arrange the images to fit the paper and then print out the digital board so you can post it where you will see it each day.

Digital Vision Boards

If you like the idea of the vision board but don't want to print and/or post them then you can build a digital version. Several options for this are:

- Create your digital vision board within Google Docs or Evernote, or a similar app, so you can have access to it from everywhere you go.

    o The Evernote app (or something similar) is an amazing way to file, access, and share anything on the go. This app allows you to save all kinds of media (images, videos, text, and music) so you can create a Vision board folder full of pieces that remind you of what you are working towards.

Special note: Remember that if you choose a digital vision board approach that you need to create a habit in the morning and/or other times throughout the day, to look through it. By doing this regularly you are more likely to stay on track and to align your daily decisions with your goals.

Mind-body Connections

Humans have known for centuries there is a strong connection between our mind and our body. There have been sayings around for centuries like: I have a gut feeling, butterflies in my stomach, shivers down my spine, weak in the knees, and many others. Prior to scientific breakthroughs in the 1800s, most people understood that emotions and thoughts would and did affect a person's health. They believed that positive emotions could help heal and alleviate illness, while negative emotions and thought patterns could manifest disease and negative conditions. Once science uncovered information about bacteria, viruses, and anti-biotics the focus, especially in Western Societies, was to increase the use of antibiotics to treat the body and there was less focus on the mind and the person as a whole being.

In recent years the importance of treating the whole person including their thoughts and emotions has resurfaced as part of the health and healing process. Today, most people, including doctors, acknowledge there are powerful mind-body connections in which your emotional, mental, social, spiritual, and behavioral habits can affect your health. This resurgence on holistic (the whole being) medicine has ignited a flood of scientific studies on how this all works together in each human. Results from many different studies around the world show that including psychological, social and behavioral factors when treating the body can reduce pain, manage stress and anxiety and aid in treating heart disease, cancer, and many other conditions.

The brain is connected to the body through the spinal cord, muscles, cardiovascular system, and digestive tract. Each of these can send messages to the brain for processing. Here is how scientists have described the process:

There are 5 types of stimuli that the mind receives:

1. Conceptual - Based on mental activity (your thoughts).

2. Emotion - A feeling created from circumstances, or relationships with others (feeling sad, happy, and fearful, etc.).

3. Exteroception - The awareness of environmental stimuli acting on your body. (like feeling heat and cold.)

4. Interoceptive - Stimuli that arises from within your body (like stomach cramps or headaches, and your gut feelings/intuition).

5. Proprioception – The awareness of the position and movement of your body within space (like knowing you are sitting instead of standing).

Any and all of these stimuli are sent to your brain. Your brain then interprets the stimulus based on your experiences, your personality, and your mindset. It is at that moment you begin to think. When you think, you put meaning onto the stimulus that just occurred and you create a feeling about that stimulus. At the moment your brain acknowledges your thoughts about the experience, it releases chemicals into your body to react to the stimulus. So, your feeling is directly based on the meaning you have created related to the stimulus and how that fits into your perception of life. You cannot think happy thoughts and be sad, and you cannot think sad thoughts and be happy. You also cannot think angry thoughts and feel peaceful. Your thoughts actually create your emotion since once you create the meaning in your mind. Your body then releases the related chemicals which affect your moods.

Happy Chemicals

I mentioned above that our body releases chemicals based on our thoughts. Let's explore that a little. If we have chemicals that make us feel different emotions, what chemicals help make us feel happy? How are they created? What can we do to create more of those more often?

Below is a rundown of the four chemicals we create that are commonly called our "Happy Chemicals."

Dopamine

The happiness you feel when you buy a new home or get a promotion, make a great meal, find a solution to a problem, or learn something new is the result of a dopamine surge. A rush of dopamine is released each time we reach an achievement or overcome a challenge. This makes us feel great and motivates us to take action toward other goals, desires, and needs to create a new surge of dopamine.

Ways to generate dopamine in your body:

Take on new challenges and make note of each step you take toward achieving them every day! This consistent achievement in forward motion will also consistently release dopamine, making you feel proud of your accomplishments and feel happy with yourself! This is the reason it can feel so good to mark items off of your to-do list. The acknowledgment you have completed the task releases a dopamine rush of pleasure!

Serotonin

Serotonin flows when you feel significant or important. When you acknowledge you have made a difference in someone's life, contributed to an important cause, or been acknowledged for something positive that you did.

Ways to generate serotonin in your body:

Think about all the good you contribute to your relationships and the world around you. Acknowledge your importance (to your family, your children, your pet, your friends, your work, your community, and the world). Take a moment and visualize your achievements and victories in your mind. Whether they are from five minutes ago or five years ago, visualize what happened, what you were wearing, where you were, how you felt? This allows you to relive the experience in your mind. Your body will react to the thought stimulus and produce serotonin. This visualization can be done anywhere.

Activity: *Another way to use the visualization technique is to visualize future experiences and achievements as if you have already completed or attained them. If there is something in your life you want to achieve, visualize yourself already having completed it and how great you will feel.*

Imagine every detail as if you were watching a movie in your mind. Feel the emotions like you have achieved your goal (sometimes my visions will even bring me to happy tears). Besides feeling good you will likely feel even more motivated to actually move closer to your goal!

This visualization technique is used by successful athletes worldwide. In addition to their regular practice routines, they visualize themselves winning over and over so it becomes the natural outcome. It works for them, and will work for you.

Moderate daily exposure to some sunshine will also promote serotonin (and vitamin D) production. Open up your window coverings, sit by a sunny window, take a walk/run/bike ride outside, do some gardening, even just stand outside to stretch, or go for a pleasant drive during the day. Any behavior that allows your body to soak up a mild amount of sunlight will help generate a positive mood.

Oxytocin

Oxytocin creates feelings of intimacy and trust to help us build healthy relationships. It is often called the "cuddle hormone," because it is important in creating strong bonds with others. Therefore, it makes sense this is the chemical released by men and women during orgasm and by mothers during childbirth or breastfeeding since these are important bonding moments.

Other ways to generate Oxytocin in your body:

- Be a hugger. Positive touch can be an instant Oxytocin booster.

- Be a giver. When you give a gift and see the other person's happy response it raises the oxytocin level in you and in the person that received the gift. Serotonin levels can rise since receiving the gift can make the person feel special and important and their reaction to receiving the gift can make you feel special and important. Donating to a cause is another great way to give.

- Be a smiler. This small, no-cost gesture is so simple and yet has been proven to have miraculous positive effects on people.

Endorphins

Endorphins are released to minimize feelings of stress, fear, or pain and alleviate anxiety and depression. They also can be released if triggered with a stimulus that is somewhat dangerous but enjoyable to the individual. For example if you like riding a roller coaster, bungee jumping, skiing downhill fast, or surfing on the ocean waves you will experience a rush of pleasure during these moments.

Other ways to generate endorphins in your body:

Eating chili peppers, having pleasurable sex, taking a cold shower, or giving birth to a child can generate endorphins. Exercise can also create a surge of endorphins (the "Runner's High") and treatments like acupuncture and massage can also release the natural chemical. Endorphin pleasure is powerful and can drive you to repeat behaviors that give you the endorphin surge. If left unchecked these behaviors can become excessive and manifest as addictions.

Being aware of the mind-body connection empowers you with the knowledge to engage in activities that generate your happy chemicals to create positive feelings and sensations in your body. The next step is to incorporate positive habits into your daily life.

More ways to generate your happy chemicals:

- Smile, laugh, act silly, dance, sing
- Ride a roller coaster, anything really fast
- Take a cold shower
- Get exposed to mild sunlight
- Get massage therapy or acupuncture, Reiki
- Do yoga, meditation, deep breathing exercises
- Give lots of hugs and compliments

- Tell people you love that you love them
- Be grateful and give thanks
- Say positive daily affirmations out loud
- Have loving, fun sex
- Become a part of a cause bigger than yourself
- Do things you can be proud of
- Write to-do lists, complete the items and mark them off when done
- Give and be generous to others
- Set goals and achieve them
- Take a class and/or learn something new
- Pet an animal
- Relive happy memories
- Listen to music (or play it if you have that talent)
- Be creative: art, writing, sewing, music, cooking, dancing, etc.
- Search for treasure - bargain shopping, searching music from your past or for the perfect recipe, collecting, geocaching, scavenger hunts, etc.

Activity: Create your own "Happy Book."
Only include items that make you feel happy:

- List memories
- Compliments you were given
- Accomplishments
- Awards
- Certifications
- Cards / letters

The benefits of Your Happy Book:

- First, creating it and adding to it allows you to acknowledge the good things that happen and the contributions and accomplishments you make.

- Second, to add good things, you first must become aware of the good things happening in your life. The more you look for them, the more you will find.

- Third, the writing process (even just little notes, etc.) can bring such a sense of freedom and release. It is so empowering to write down your thoughts. Writing can bring clarity to you and feelings of gratitude toward yourself and others.

- Fourth, whenever you are feeling low, you can turn to this book and review all these wonderful things that make you feel good about yourself! Your happy chemicals will kick in and you will feel a sense of pride and happiness.

A Happy Diet

A Happy Diet includes happy chemical producing foods like these:

Almonds	Nuts
Apples	Oatmeal
Avocados	Olive oil
Bananas	Oregano
Beets & beetroot	Rosemary
Coffee	Sea vegetables
Dark chocolate	Sesame or pumpkin seeds
Eggs	Soy products
Fish	Spicy peppers
Green leafy vegetables	Turmeric
Green tea	Watermelon
Lima beans	Wheat germ

Body Language

Did you know that your body language not only reflects to others an image of who you are but actually can affect your own feelings and perceptions of who you are! This means that by changing even simple things like your posture, the way you sit, move, or hold your head can make you actually feel more happy and optimistic!

Does that sound crazy? Well, consider this; have you ever walked past a large mirror or window and seen your reflection walking along hunched over? Did you immediately straighten up? In that moment when you changed from walking hunched over to walking upright, did you feel better? Like you were walking with purpose? Maybe even lighter and happier? These feelings may not have lasted all day, but for those few moments, your posture change also affected a change in your mood.

So here are a few other ways to use our body-mind connections to create positivity quickly through our body language. When you feel a limiting emotion, acknowledge it, say to yourself, "I am feeling_____ (angry, sad, discouraged, jealous, etc.). Then take a moment to notice your posture and make a change:

- Stand up/sit-up straighter.

- Put your shoulders back.

- Look up.

- Take longer steps / quicken your pace.

- Laugh out loud (if appropriate).

- Run or dance in place.

- Take three deep breaths (and smile).

- Just smile (look in the mirror if you can) – hold your smile for as long as you can – the longer you smile at yourself the better you will feel and you may even laugh.

- Be Grateful – Take a moment to think about something or someone you are grateful to have in your life. You can even say thank you out loud to yourself which will reinforce and intensify your feeling of gratitude in that moment.

Action

Although reading, researching, learning, dreaming, and visualizing are great ways to absorb knowledge, gain new perspectives, and even open your mind to new opportunities and activities available to you, to create the fabulous life you dream of, you must act. To meet new people, to go to new places, and do new things, you must "go" and "do".

Nothing will teach you faster or move your life forward in ways bigger than taking action. We learn more by doing and processing the outcomes to our actions than we do from conceptualizing things.

A good example of this is if you think about learning how to use a new computer program or app on your phone. You can read about the program and even view the tutorials but until you actually take action and use the program you will not understand the benefits it gives you or how it works. That is like everything in life. My daughter recently got her driver's permit. She studied driving for the written test but had never been behind the wheel. She obviously had observed people driving her whole life, but when she got behind the wheel for the first time it was all very different, exciting, and scary to her. She learned so much more about driving from being in the driver's seat than from studying or riding along as a passenger. You are the driver of your life.

I know sometimes our life takes turns we may not have expected and that can knock us down but you can redirect your life to keep it (or get it back) on course. All success in anything is caused by taking action.

The other thing about actually doing things is that it will raise your confidence and will ignite a fire within you by setting off all of your happy chemicals. When you accomplish goals and overcome challenges, it makes you feel good about yourself. The key here is to do things that will make you proud once you have done them, not things you will regret later. Fear is the number one thing that can hold you back from having, doing, or being the person you want to be, with the life you want to live. When you take risks and overcome your fears, you are rewarded with, among other things, pride. Pride in oneself is a magnificent thing because it propels you on with confidence to tackle and accomplish more.

Coming out of a relationship is hard. You may need a confidence boost after the changes that have occurred in your life. So take action toward some new idea. Do it now. There is no need to wait since time will continue to pass and you would rather look back saying "Wow, look what I have done," than to still be sitting around thinking about what would happen if you did do it.

Activity: Start with the end in mind. You can use this technique for anything really: losing weight, planning a party, getting a new job, buying a home, or making new friends. It is a powerful tool to get clear on action steps to create the life you want to live!

Take a moment and just let yourself dream about what you want your life to look and feel like. Seriously visualize your life so clearly that you can feel your response to it. When you can feel the happiness and the energy from your vision, it becomes that much more certain that your vision will become your reality. So now let's take this further, beyond this first stage of wanting. To do this, ask yourself this question,

"Based on the dream I have for my life, what would have to be true for that to be my reality?"
Now write down what comes to mind. Each time you answer, "Well, I would need to... (have, do, or be...)." Then, based on that answer, ask yourself the same question again. Keep asking yourself that same question, about each answer you come up with. "What would have to be true for that to be my reality?"

Keep going in this manner until you have connected where you are today with your new vision of reality. You have just created the path to get you what you want! That is so exciting! So now you have created a path of what you must have, do, or be to make your dream your reality.

Take the actions required to get you to each next step and you will create your dream life. Start today. There is no reason to wait.

The Five-second Rule

"5-4-3-2-1… Go!" Have you heard of Mel Robbins? *Her 5 Second Rule* is a powerful tactic (and book) to help change your life by changing the way you approach doing new things. Sometimes trying something new or taking action to accomplish a pending task can be hard.

Here is how to overcome that hesitation, in the words of Mel Robbins:

> "The moment you feel yourself hesitate (when you know you should do something) start counting backwards 5-4-3-2-1, then say GO. The Rule is a proven, form of metacognition. When you use it, you shift mental gears, interrupt your habit of overthinking and awaken your pre-frontal cortex – making change easy. The rule acts as a "starting ritual" that breaks bad habits and triggers positive new behavior change."

https://melrobbins.com/5-second-rule/

As we have all heard before, the first step is the hardest. If we just start, we will gain momentum and that momentum will continue to push us forward. Having a personal mental ritual can remind us to move forward. Not just with exercise, or our career, or our relationships, or our finances… but all of it. As you create this new you and move toward your goals, there will undoubtedly be moments where you feel yourself hesitating. You had a brilliant idea pop into your head and then you hesitated. The longer you hesitate the more your mind talks you out of the great idea or starts to minimize the importance of your idea. Instead, create an action you can do with that great idea right now and then just like Mel Robbins says, count 5-4-3-2-1 and Go!

Now, I understand there are many instances when ideas will pop into our heads and we cannot act on it at that very moment. What I have learned to do during those times is to make my immediate action toward that idea as simple as – writing it down, or recording it into my phone voice app or even text it to myself or leave myself a voice message or enter it onto my calendar – something so that when I have time I can go back to it and then take another step in the right direction. That may be developing a plan, making a phone call, researching a topic, writing a list, meeting someone, creating something, anything that keeps your action headed toward bringing your idea into reality.

Personal Mantra

Another tool I use to coach myself at times of stress is a personal mantra. This is a phrase that makes you feel empowered and reduces your stress. You repeat or chant this mantra to yourself (in your head or out loud) when you need a quick reminder of how awesome you are! I actually have a few I use depending on the situation.

The ones I use most often are:

- "I am pure Joy." Since this is my name, it reminds me to be authentic to whom I am, it also reminds me I want to be in a Joyful mindset full of gratitude and that I can bring joy to others with kindness and inspiration.

- "Just do it." This old Nike slogan is so great as a reminder to act. It has worked for me often to overcome fear. Whether it be going on a date, speaking in front of large groups of people, or starting a new goal, we all must "Just do it."

- "Who cares?" Now I know this may seem like a negative phrase so I want to explain how I use it in a positive way. For me, what I am reminding myself of is that I need not let a fear of what others think stop me from doing what I want to do. If I am doing something that will make me feel proud and move my life forward in the direction I want, then others opinions of me don't matter. Now I want to specify here I am talking about the masses of people. There are people close to you, friends and family, that may help guide you and you may care what they think. This mantra is not used for me to go run amuck and not care about the repercussions of my actions on others but it empowers me to do what is right for me with courage and kindness to others.

New Paths

One easy way to jumpstart your new life and move away from the memories of the past is to look at your world in new ways. Take the opportunity to shift your everyday environments whenever you can. The key is to disrupt your routines. You never know what or who you may find on a new path! Here are a few simple strategies to support you in maintaining your positive mindsets and creating new possibilities:

- Walk or drive to work/school a different way
- Try new restaurants
- Go to different malls/stores
- Take different hiking/biking trails
- Go to a different park
- Drive down different streets

New Places

Whether local or far, travel to new places. This could be the next city over or across the globe. Engaging with new environments, people, foods, and cultures (you can find many cultures represented within and across the United States). The point is to go to new places. If you can travel, GO! Head to somewhere exciting and that you have been wanting to visit. Travel always provides us the opportunity to broaden our perspectives and to feel grateful for our opportunities. It is also a way to meet fascinating people. It is never too early to check things off of our bucket lists!

If you are concerned about traveling alone, grab a friend and go, or look into travel groups. Many companies specialize in travel tours, some specifically for singles, and more companies are catering to single women travelers and the economic power we possess.

Here are some very telling statistics from The Gutsy Traveler Website (AAA Girlfriend Travel Research Project #070005 March 2017). Just reading these may help you to get more comfortable with beginning, or continuing, a globetrotter lifestyle as part of your new life!

- There has been a 230% increase in the number of women-only travel companies since 2011.

- The average adventure traveler is a 47-year-old female.

- About 4% of all U.S. annual travel spending (almost $200 million per year) is from women traveling with other women.

- Since 2014, about 24% of women in the U.S. have traveled with another woman for a girlfriend getaway.

- Approximately 39% of American women are planning a girlfriend trip by 2020.

- Women make up 75% of those who take cultural, adventure or nature trips.

New People

The reality of a breakup or divorce is that the people you had in your life during your relationship/marriage will change. You may still see many of the same people, but the unfortunate truth is that people that knew both of you will align more with one of you. Not everyone will consciously want this to happen but they will find it easier to align with only one of you as they hear stories from both of you and feel in the middle. You also will feel different around many folks and not as comfortable sharing things happening in your new life. Knowing these things happen may not make it easier when they do, but since this book is about dealing with change in a positive way for you to move forward into your dreams, here are a few things to consider:

Don't limit yourself only to the people and/or groups you knew before you were single. This is a time where all good things are expanding with you. Think about the type of people you want to bring into your new community of friends, associates, lovers, etc. Take a moment and visualize yourself surrounded by these people. How do you feel? Great, right? We all must expand our tribes of people we feel great around! And they need you too! When we are alive from pursuing things that make us happy our contribution also expands and instead of a "vicious circle" of bad thoughts and feelings, we can create a "victorious circle" of feeling great which radiates out and touches others making them feel great too!

Consider who is on your "team". This is an important concept to think about as you emerge from the relationship you were in and become true to your New Self. Are the people you associate with supporting you, brainstorming with you, excited about your future... "On your team?" This life transition gives you the opportunity to do things differently - be selective about what and who you now add to your life. There may be people from your past that don't understand the transformation you are making. They may not comprehend the struggles and achievements that you are going through... that doesn't mean you have to kick them off the team entirely – maybe they just need to be benched for a while. Have faith in your gut as you talk to old friends and new friends. Look for those that you can support and those that will support you.

One of the great things about the internet is that it has made it easier to bring like-minded people together. Here are a few ways you can meet the new people you dream about...

- Classes
- Clubs
- Leagues
- Workplace
- Kids sporting events
- Travel
- Camping
- Business Networking
- Organizations/associations
- Alumni Events
- Single Parent Groups
- Divorce Support Groups
- Bereavement Support Groups

Meetup.com

Meetup.com is a website that was co-founded in 2002 by Scott Heiferman and Brendan McGovern when the two were inspired by the people of New York coming together after the attacks on 9-11-2001. It is a website that enables people to engage with others in groups based on shared interests and goals.

Their mission as stated on their website:

> "Meetup brings people together in thousands of cities to do more of what they want to do in life. It is organized around one simple idea: when we get together and do the things that matter to us, we're at our best. And that's what Meetup does.

It brings people together to do, explore, teach and learn the things that help them come alive."

Through groups on Meetup.com, I have: hiked, kayaked, paddle boarded, sailed, surfed, biked, danced, wine tasted, camped, dined, gone to concerts, plays, movies, pumpkin patches, picnics, New Year Eve celebrations, attended discussions about philosophy, science, politics, finances, business, beauty, yoga, motivation, books, cooking, foreign languages, and more.

I have learned about activities and places in my own city I was not aware even existed and I have met people I would have never met without going to a meetup.com group event.

There are also groups just for women to get together and connect with social activities, single parent groups that get the parent and the children involved in fun activities, pet groups, cooking groups, writing groups, book clubs and singles groups for every age bracket. A great thing about Meetup.com is that if the group you want does not exist, you can easily create it. Become an organizer and start your group by building the group profile, mission, and calendar. People with the same interests will find you and join you and you can start your "tribe." Have fun with this! Meeting new people and doing fun things you enjoy will be the foundation of happiness for you in your life.

A list of your interests and desires you create will help guide you closer to the people and experiences you have identified as exciting to you. This is big. So let's take action on this one right now.

Activity: Make a list of your interests and desires. This will guide you closer to the people and experiences you have identified as exciting to you.

"What have I always wanted to try doing?" Write all the things that come to mind, now ask, "What do I miss doing that I have not done in a while?" Write all those things down.

Now, write down at least fifty more things you want to do that maybe you have never thought about before. It may seem difficult to think of fifty things, but you can do it! Things like sports activities, types of foods you want to eat, books you want to read, classes you want to take, languages you want to learn, planning a trip, anything you have an interest in...

If you have children I also recommend you make a second list - think about the things you want to do with them. Ask them what new things they want to do, involve them in making a list with you of things you can all try together. This is so fun and leads to some great experiences and new memories with them.

Nature

Nature is defined as everything that has not been created by humankind including plants, insects, animals, mountains, rocks, oceans, sunshine, clouds, the moon and stars. When you connect with these elements by being present to what is around you, you can feel rejuvenated.

Throughout history nature has intrigued people from all over the world. Leonardo da Vinci, Ralph Waldo Emmerson, Henry David Thoreau, and Albert Einstein repeatedly praised nature and believed that nature was the source for all knowledge about our universe.

Scientists today continually uncover more and more details that show the huge impact nature has on every one of us. Multiple studies from all over the globe have found that when people consciously connect with nature they feel happier, more positive, more energetic, and healthier. Even a few minutes a day walking through a park or gazing up at the sky or trees, or ocean can improve your focus and your frame of mind both in the moment and after. Physical ailments like respiratory tract and cardiovascular illnesses can be helped by experiencing nature because of the direct effects it has on lowering the blood pressure, heart rate, and the production of stress hormones. The exposure to sunshine also helps to generate happy chemicals within your body and the beauty of the sky, plants, rocks, clouds, and colors can touch your soul.

We live on a magnificent planet. If you are feeling overwhelmed and stressed, sad, hopeless, anxious or any array of negative feelings, then please arrange to somehow get out of your surroundings for a walk, bike ride, hike, swim, boat ride, kayak, paddle board, camping trip, or anything outdoors. A drive or train ride through trees, open spaces, or along the coast can be exhilarating. Even just sitting outside quietly on a chair, park bench, rock, or ground will work. The key is to stay off your phone, look up and around, roll your windows down (if applicable) and feel the breeze on your skin. I cannot emphasize enough how important getting outside is to promote and maintain your happy state of mind.

Nature is so powerful that studies have even shown that looking out a window at plants or even at an image of a scene in nature can have an uplifting effect, improve focus, and can even help people with injuries heal quicker.

Here is a list of some of the many health benefits to be had from your connection with nature.

Special note: This list has been compiled during my research on the effects of nature. Although it may seem long, it is nowhere near complete.

- Increases energy level
- Increases quality of sleep
- Increases feeling of happiness
- Increases sense of purpose
- Increases sense of belonging
- Increases empathy
- Increases ability to focus

- Increases immunity
- Increases speed of recovery from surgery/ illness
- Increases lifespan
- Reduces depression
- Reduces fear
- Reduces stress
- Reduces anger
- Reduces anxiety
- Reduces mental fatigue
- Reduces violence and aggression
- Reduces blood pressure
- Reduces heart rate
- Reduces muscle tension
- Reduces symptoms of ADHD
- Reduces the production of stress hormones
- Reduces hypertension (abnormally high blood pressure)
- Reduces respiratory tract illnesses
- Reduces cardiovascular illnesses

We are undeniably connected with nature. Use this insight as a tool in your mood toolbox and enjoy nature as often as you can. It is free to everyone and will reap huge rewards in all phases of your life.

Support

There are many support services available today. Each type can provide you with support, new perspectives, and knowledge to move you forward in your life.

Since you will go through many phases during your life, you may want to engage in these relationships at different times. It is not uncommon to have engaged with many types of support specialist as we move throughout our lives and achievements. Many people do not realize there are so many options and even if you know of them, you may not know the distinct differences. Which type is best for you right now? To help you decide, here is information on each type of support service relationship so you will be best informed to decide what is best for you.

Therapist/Counselor

This commonly referred to "traditional" support professional focuses on dealing with healing pain and dysfunction arising from your past. You share thoughts and feelings about your current and past life events with the therapist/counselor to help resolve upsets and difficulties affecting your current emotional state and to develop healthy ways to deal with your present life situations.

There are many specialties available when looking for a therapist or counselor. It can get confusing when reviewing credentials since each professional can have numerous credential acronyms listed by their name. I have listed a few common credential acronyms below for your easy reference to ensure you find the best match for you.

LCDC	Licensed Chemical Dependency Counselor
LCMHC	Licensed Clinical Mental Health Counselor
LMFT	Licensed Marriage and Family Therapist
LPC	Licensed Professional Counselor
MFCC	Marriage, Family and Child Counselor
MFT	Marriage and Family Therapist
NCC	National Certified Counselor
NCPsyA	Nationally Certified Psychoanalyst
NCSC	National Certified School Counselor
RPC	Registered Professional Counselor
SAP	Substance Abuse Professional
SW	Social Worker

Follow this link if you would like to review a full list: https://www.networktherapy.com/directory/credentials.asp

Consultant

Consultants are generally hired to analyze situations and then provide recommendations for change and the execution of plans to facilitate the change. They are expert in a particular topic and will typically tell you what to do based on their background then, you follow their lead.

Consultants are very effective with business situations or diet and exercise, any situation where you might want to receive and follow a customized plan for you developed by someone else.

Mentor

A mentor is someone who has been in a similar situation as you and shares knowledge from their learnings and experiences related to the specific area. They may share processes, ask and answer questions and provide recommendations based on their experiences and interpretations to your specific needs.

Professional Trainer

Professional training is usually organized around a specific objective. The programs are created and conducted in a consistent manner for each individual and/or group. This type of training is often used in professional certification programs. The curriculum walks you through a step by step process toward a single defined goal. The result is expected to deliver the same knowledge to all participants.

Life Coach

The life coach will exhibit many of the same characteristics described above but there are some distinct differences between life coaching and the others.

- The life coach client (not patient) is emotionally stable and focused on creating a future (not focused on resolving the past as with a therapist/counselor).

- Life coaching sessions occur with the belief that the individual (or group) can generate their own answers and solutions for challenges and/or questions that come up for them. Therefore, a life coach will not provide the answers (like a mentor, consultant, or trainer) but will enable and inspire you to develop your own solutions to reach your objectives.

The life coaching session focuses on the client's defined topic, establishes action steps, and confirms accountability agreements to enable and support the client in reaching their goals. The results do not happen in a step by step process. They can arise at different times throughout the session discussion and may connect with other areas of the client's life. This leads the client to re-evaluate previous plans and opportunities.

The life coach asks powerful questions and uses supportive and discovery-based approaches to cause the client to think and see information from new perspectives. This leads to an opening up of possibilities for the client that they did not see from their previous viewpoints. Seeing new self-realized possibilities creates expansion, energy, and excitement for the client which motivates them to create and implement plans to achieve their desired results.

Starting/Re-Starting Your Career

Whether you are starting your career or re-entering the workforce, take a moment to stop and think about what you *want* to do. Today there are so many types of jobs, types of organizations and types of work cultures. Many people just automatically assume that they want job "X" because they don't know there are other options open to them.

Think big. Depending on your financial situation, this may also be a great time to start a business of your own, write a book, consult, speak, etc. Be open to thinking and acting in new ways. You deserve everything you want to have, do, and be, there is a big world out there.

Be open to opportunities that present themselves to you as you go through this process. Even if you encounter opportunities you did not expect, note to yourself if they excite you, and are aligned with your life vision. If they are, act upon them!

Activity: Create a "word list." Write down at least 25 things you like and/or are passionate about. You could even go back to the list you did in the "New People" section for inspiration. This list can help guide you as you begin your search for your career.

Research

Once you have your word list (see activity above), use the words as keywords to search on Google, on business sites like MSN money, Yahoo Finance, Forbes, CNBC, and on job post sites like Monster.com. Read through the search results. It is fascinating to read about some of the creative businesses out there and how much the business cultures vary by company, industry, region, etc.

For any companies you are interested working for, sign up for their marketing emails and/or their investor relations notifications so you keep updated on the latest news. Being an empowered woman stems from having information and creating options for yourself. The more you can know about the business world, and your passions, the more success you will have in finding and/or creating a job that will align with your needs and life vision.

Training

Career Coaching

There are many highly effective career coaches with a mission to help women with their career goals. These coaches can offer you customized, one-on-one services for things like writing your resume, connecting you with industry contacts, identifying your personality types, and locating job openings that are good fits for you. To find them, start by searching online for "career coach" in your area.

Key considerations when selecting a career coach:

- Do they have experience in your industry of interest?

- Do they have relevant business connections to help you network?

- Do they empower you in achieving your vision?

Returnship Programs

There are also many companies out there that offer training programs for people re-entering the workplace. They each offer different systems of support and some specialize in specific industries. Benefits gained from working with these companies includes: the relationships they have with a network of companies to place people into job roles, the knowledge they have about the skills you will need, and the resources they have to train you effectively.

Here are several of the most well-known companies and a short quote from their website:

- **irelaunch.com** – "iRelaunch is the leader in career reentry programming of all kinds. iRelaunch works directly with over 30 blue chip companies in a range of roles, to develop, pilot, source for, present in and publicize their reentry internship programs, or similarly support their efforts to hire relaunchers directly into open roles without internships."

- **onrampfellowship.com** – "The Fellowship is a re-entry platform that matches experienced lawyers returning to the workforce with top organizations for six month and one-year paid positions."

- **pathforward.org** – "Path Forward is a nonprofit organization on a mission to empower people to restart their careers after time spent focused on caregiving."

- **reachire.com** – "reacHIRE is dedicated to moving business forward by bringing women back. Through comprehensive recruiting, training and placement programs that support diverse hiring, we give companies an alternative channel for tapping into a powerful, underutilized talent pool - returning women."

- **rebootaccel.com** – "ReBoot Accel offers a suite of programs to get women current, connected, and confident to return to the workforce or pursue new goals."

- **thesecondshift.com** – "The Second Shift gives professional women a clear path to remain in the workforce when full-time employment is not an option. We enable companies to retain critical female voices, influence, and expertise in the workplace."

Basic Skills

Regardless of what direction you want to pursue, there are skills you will need. Do not wait to begin your learning process, start today. Many of these things will be an advantage to you throughout your life in any career or personal setting. Here are basic things everyone should become proficient in:

- **Email:** If you do not have a professional sounding email or are not using email much right now, you must set up an account to begin sending and receiving your professional messages. You can easily set up a free account at Outlook.com or Gmail.com. Do not create email addresses that you think are funny or creative. Keep your professional email address simple with some form of your first and last name and/or initials. You will be including this on your resumes and professional inquiries so you want it to be easy and straightforward.

- **Online calendar systems:** These systems allow users to log events, meetings, holidays, etc. into an online calendar format that can be shared with others to manage team/group schedules. (Google calendar, iCalendar, Microsoft® Outlook calendar, etc.) These programs and/or apps can be a powerful way for you, your family, or groups to plan and share schedules and are widely used in many businesses.

- **Conference calling:** A call in which several people all are joined simultaneously for listening and/or conversation. Since many teams have members at different locations, conference calls happen regularly at most businesses. If you want to get more familiar with how these work, or set up your own call-in number, you can search on "conference call services" and/or visit FreeConferenceCalls.com

- **Web meetings:** A virtual meeting where multiple people come together with both audio and visual components to present, share, and collaborate. Some commonly used services are WebEx.com, GoToMeeting.com, and Zoom.us

- **Microsoft Office:** For years the Microsoft Windows operating system and the Microsoft Office suite powered over 90% of all computers worldwide. Times are changing, but these main four programs are still important to know:

  1) Microsoft® Word: A word processing program used to write and format documents for essays, reports, proposals, etc.

  2) Microsoft® Excel: A spreadsheet program used for calculating numbers with built-in formats and formulas.

  3) Microsoft® PowerPoint: A presentation graphics program used to create slides for slideshow presentations. It can incorporate multiple types of media (text, images, video, and sound) on the slides to create engaging "decks" for presentations.

  4) Microsoft® Outlook: A personal information managers and communications program that contains e-mail, contacts, tasks, and calendars.

Special note: Microsoft ® Office for Windows includes additional programs listed below. The office suite for

Mac computers is limited to the main four shown above: Word, Excel, PowerPoint, and Outlook.

Depending on what you will be doing, you may also want to learn a few others.

1. *Access: Database management program*

2. *Lync: Collaboration and communication tool*

3. *OneNote: Note taking program*

4. *Project: Project management programs and solutions*

5. *Publisher: Business publishing and marketing materials program*

6. *Visio: Business and technical diagramming program*

- **Google Docs:** A competitor to Microsoft® Office, Google Docs allows users to create text documents, slide presentations, spreadsheets, drawings, and surveys. It has powerful online collaboration tools that provide multiple users access to share and edit the same document in real-time. Google Docs is the system of choice for many of the United States schools and is continuing to grow in popularity within business communities as well.

Special note: Tutorials are available to help you learn many of these programs. Search online for "Tutorial...for the program you want to learn". You can search on any search engine and/or directly on YouTube.com since many tutorials will be in video formats to help explain the tools better.

- **Negotiation Skills:** Negotiations happen all the time in business and in life so be aware of some basic negotiation components. You will want to practice these skills when considering job offers from prospective employers, partners, and/or vendors to negotiate the best options for you to reach your goals.

  o Know your strengths in the situation: What does the other person want? How do you provide it? What makes you unique?

  o Determine what the key drivers are for the other person's agenda and emphasize you as a solution to these needs. Are they in a rush? Do they have limited resources/money? Do they need a person with very specific qualifications?

  o Be prepared to ask for more than what you feel would be an acceptable compensation package so you have built-in leverage to compromise by giving up some things.

Special note: Whenever you give up something don't be afraid to ask for something in return. For example, if they can't give you the salary you want, ask if they can give you more paid vacation, flexible schedules, a sign on bonus, commissions, or stock options, etc.

  o Always listen; never interrupt when negotiating. Since you don't know what the person will say next, let them completely finish before you speak. They may get around to saying exactly what you want to hear, or sometimes they may offer options even better than you had imagined. Silence is one of the most powerful skills to have in negotiations. Once you have asked a question or stated an important point, stop talking and just wait (this works in person as well as over phone, text or email). Sometimes the silence can be painful and scary but wait it out to see how they will answer. This is a great habit to form for any important conversation.

o   Know the least you will accept going into the negotiation. If they offer you more than you expected you can be decisive and confident in a quick decision. If they offer you less, you will know immediately that you need to negotiate further to get to a package that will make you happy.

Networking

If you do not already have a profile on Linked in set it up immediately. If you do already have one, update it.

- Ensure you have a profile photo that is recent and professional looking. Do not upload a photo that is fuzzy or too casual and definitely not a selfie. It should be a headshot showing shoulders and up in a professional shirt, dress, or suit.

- Be active on LinkedIn. Search, post, and message people asking them to endorse your skills and/or write recommendations for you.

- Connect with people you know to expand your network both offline and online.

- Make sure your privacy settings allow for recruiters to find you. (Go to your profile photo icon, click "Settings and Privacy" then click on "Privacy" at the top. Now scroll down to "Job seeking preferences")

Many people get so involved with online networking and social media that they forget physical networking is critical too. Talk with people you know about your job search; Ask if they know anyone connected to the industries and/or jobs you are seeking. Find out about any jobs they know of and what topics they recommend you know about, the current state of the industry, competitors, the company cultures, skills, and any associations/organizations you should be a part of. Then take those nuggets of information and do the research to build your knowledge in those areas.

Your Resume

Your resume is your personal advertisement. The person that receives it will likely not know you so it is the content in your resume that must get you the interview. You want the reader to be able to envision you in the role as they discover more about you.

Resume Format

Pick a resume template for your document. You can find many Resume Templates online for free. There are three main styles: Reverse-chronological, Functional, or Combination.

- The reverse-chronological format focuses on your work experience timeline (from most recent to oldest) and documents your career history with details about your roles, responsibilities, and accomplishments.

- A functional resume highlights your key skills and accomplishments without a timeline structure. You can convey your personal skills in a professional way organized by role or function instead of dates.

- A combination format can put your relevant qualifications, accomplishments, and skills first and then include a brief section on your career history later.

Special note: Since a reverse chronological format will emphasize any time gaps in your career history, if you are new to the work-world or re-entering after a leave, use a Functional or Combination resume style instead. These formats will better highlight your strengths and talents instead of accentuating any time gaps.

Resume Content

Before you begin writing, take a moment to re-read the description of the job you are applying for. Your resume should align with the qualities listed in the description for the position. Use some of the same key words from the description to mirror back to them that you have the characteristics and skills they are looking for.

Special note: You can also study employment postings for similar jobs to get to know the industry buzz words or desired qualifications for comparable positions. Search for similar job titles on sites like Monster.com or Indeed.com to find additional samples for review.

Always customize your resume a bit for each job you apply for so that it resonates with the person who reads it. Do not create one resume and send it out to multiple companies or for multiple job roles. Use your original version as a template and then modify it as needed based on each of the job descriptions you are applying for.

- Keep your entire resume document to no more than two pages.

- Your contact information should be at the top of the document. Include your name, phone number, professional email address, professional social media handles (LinkedIn and Twitter), any links to your professional websites, portfolios, or blogs but only include items that are relevant to the job you are applying for. Do not include any of your personal social account information.

- Use bulleted lists – this simplifies the look of your resume, requires fewer words/space, and allows the reviewer to see the information faster.

- Use numbers to quantify things everywhere you can: How many people did you manage in your

- previous jobs, community work, sports team management, charity involvement, school groups? Did you manage the budgets? Did you have quotas? What were the numbers?

- Include freelance work and volunteer or community roles to show your leadership, organizational, communication, strategic planning and problem-solving skills that can be applied to a professional role.

- Do not include your salary history. You can always provide it later if needed. (In some states it is illegal to ask for salary history so research online to find if this question is allowed in your state).

- Do not include references on your resume. You can provide these later too, if requested. Prepare a separate sheet with references to have handy if/when they do request it. Also make sure you notify anyone you include on your reference list so they will be prepared for a call from your prospective employer(s).

- Include any education and/or relevant certifications you have completed or are currently taking.

- Include memberships in any professional organizations and/or major conferences you have attended as long as they are relevant to this specific job application.

Resume Editing

Make sure all the information you included is relevant to the specific position you are applying for and that it is all easy to understand.

Run grammar and spell checks on the content and fix any identified errors.

Ensure the pages are formatted correctly by printing out a copy so you can proof it for errors and check the page formatting. Even if you only send a digital copy they may need to print a copy and you want it to look perfect on paper too.

Cover letter/Email

Your resume should be sent with a cover letter or email message. This should be no more than one page and be in a professional letter format. Explain why you are writing to them, what position you are applying for, and that you are excited about the opportunity. Make sure to include all of you contact information in your signature at the bottom.

Your Interview

Congratulations! You got the interview. They obviously liked what they saw on your resume, so relax and feel confident that they are interested in learning more about you.

Special note: Many companies will do a phone and/or video interview as a first step, which then can lead to an in person interview later. It really depends on the company, the position you are applying for, where you live in relation to their location, and how well you know the person already.

Regard the phone interview as seriously as an in-person meeting. Dress in your professional clothing (remember mind-body connections), sit up in a chair, and be attentive to the interviewer at all times. These steps will enable your confidence, personality, and knowledge to shine through the phone for the best possible outcome.

Here are a few additional strategies to optimize your interview results:

- Research the company you are interviewing with, especially as it relates to the role you are interviewing for. For example, if you are interviewing for an advertising role, know what their current ad campaign looks like, what are their slogans? If you are interviewing for marketing, how are they leveraging social media? What channels are they using? If you are a candidate for research and development or operations what products are they producing? If you are interviewing for leadership roles know as much about their financials as you can. Know their top competitors. If they are a public company, listen to their latest investor call (found on their website under investor relations). Also, visit their website and look at any news or press releases.

- Develop a 30-second pitch about why you are the best candidate for the job. It is likely that everyone will ask you that question.

- Practice interviewing in front of the mirror or by video recording yourself. You can also ask a friend or family member to role play your interview with you by asking you interview questions. Practice often so you will be comfortable and the interview will feel natural to you.

- Project confidence with your body language. Hold your head high, maintain eye contact and smile at the interviewer(s).

- Prepare questions to ask the interviewer(s). Your best questions will show you are knowledgeable about the company and industry, and excited about the opportunity to work for the company. The questions should be about your role responsibilities, training, and/or what a typical day/week would be like in the position. (Do not ask questions about vacation time and benefits at this stage.) Search online for "sample interview questions" to get you started.

- The last question you ask should be a "soft close" to give you some insight into how you did. Some good closing questions are:
  - Based on our discussion, will you be recommending me for the position?
  - What is our next step?
  - When will you be making a decision?

- When the discussion is over, get your interviewer's direct phone number and email for follow up, thank them for their time, and shake their hand.

Follow Up

Be sure to send a thank you to the interviewer(s) for their time. Reiterate your excitement about the opportunity and why you are a great fit for the job. This can be done via email or a card in the mail.

Job Offers

Official job offers should always be given to you in writing and include all the elements discussed as part of the employment package. Many companies will give you a verbal offer to ensure you are interested before they write up all the papers but they should follow up with a written copy. If they don't provide the offer to you in writing (it usually arrives through email), ask them for it. Make sure it includes everything you are expecting and nothing that you are not, before you sign anything.

Wealth

Building and managing your wealth is critical to your happiness. Whether you are building your wealth from scratch now or have substantial amounts of monies coming in, optimizing your assets will bring only positive results for your new life. Many women have never learned how to manage their money. It took me many years and I am still learning to this day new strategies and insights that help to build not only my knowledge, but also my estate. Here are some simple tips to help guide you in your financial journey:

To build real wealth you must include four major categories in your financial life:

1. **Income** -You must have money coming to you regularly. This can be from your job, your company, a trust, investments, spousal support, etc. The more income streams you create the better as this gives you more stability over time and will help to increase your wealth faster.

   - **Pay yourself first** - When you have a job with direct deposit, have a portion of every paycheck go to a "hidden" account which will build up over time and can be available for emergencies.

   - **Free money** - Ensure that you pay into your companies 401K and/or a private retirement account. Max out any contributions that you can get from your employer since this "free money" can add up over time.

2. **Investments** - You must invest in assets that have the potential to return money to you. These can be stocks, bonds, other business partnerships, real estate, your own business, interest from accounts, etc.

Special note: Do NOT use your retirement savings to pay for your children's college education. College is expensive, but education loans tend to have the best terms and lowest interest rates available. Take advantage of these options and maintain your momentum with your retirement fund. Your children have their whole life to make money; you will need your retirement money sooner when you exit the work force.

3. **Insurance** - You must protect all that is important and valuable to you. This will include: Health insurance, Life insurance (for you and your family), Homeowners or Renters insurance, Business insurance, etc.

4. **Tax management** – Although each state is different, typically children and homeownership are deductions that most people know to take on their yearly tax return. Explore any other deductions you might deserve since good tax management will allow you to KEEP more of the money you earn.

Special note: Everyone needs to know that by owning and working your own business, you can deduct many additional expenses. Some tax credits available to business owners are things like: cell phone contracts, mileage driven to work events/meetings, office supplies, partial or all rent/mortgage if you work from home, reimbursement to trade shows and workshops, business travel, etc. Not only do these deductions help you keep more of what you make, but starting your own business may ignite your passions and help increase your income as well!

Financial Education for Women:

There are many great books and resources out there to help build your financial prowess. More and more programs are focused on helping to educate women and children on good financial habits and strategies. Search online for programs and advisors that interest you.

Here are some that I like:

- **Daily Worth (dailyworth.com)** is "devoted to women and the topics of money, work, life, and retirement." The founder, Amanda Steinberg, also wrote the book, Worth It.

- **Dave Ramsey (daveramsey.com)** "America's trusted voice on money...Learn to budget, beat debt, & build a legacy."

- **Financial Literacy Organization for Women and Girls – FLOW (sitting-pretty.org)** "We teach women and girls how to handle their money from a position of knowledge, confidence, and financial clarity."

- **Suze Orman (suzeorman.com),** the financial guru that began educating women on finance, has many resources books, articles, podcasts available. "You are never powerful in life until you are powerful over your own money."

- **The Simple Dollar (thesimpledollar.com)** covers "strategies, tools, and products that empower you to manage debt and build wealth."

  Special note: I like the article by Mike Jelinek, "Guide to Financial Independence for Women" https://www.thesimpledollar.com/guide-to-financial-independence-for-women/

- **Wi$eUp (wiseupwomen.tamu.edu)** "a financial education program for Generation X & Y women." It is a free online course from Texas A&M University that promotes learning for financial security.

- **Women's Institute for a Secure Retirement (wiserwomen.org)** has lots of information specifically directed to women on saving, investing, and retirement planning.

- **Women's Institute for Financial Education (Wife.org)** "the oldest non-profit organization dedicated to providing financial education to women in their quest for financial independence."

Be Thoughtful.

_____

_____

_____

_____

_____

_____

_____

_____

_____

_____

_____

_____

Be Thoughtful.

Be Healthy.

"Always laugh when you can. It is cheap medicine." ~Lord Byron	"The greatest wealth is health." ~Virgil	"Your diet is a bank account. Good food choices are good investments." ~Bethenny Frankel
"A healthy outside starts on the inside." ~Unknown	"The body heals with play, the mind heals with laughter, and the spirit heals with joy." ~Proverb	"The earth is what we all have in common." ~Wendell Berry
"It is no coincidence that four of the letters in health are "heal." ~Ed Northstrum	"Nothing makes a woman more beautiful than the belief that she is beautiful." ~Sophia Loren	"A healthy lifestyle is not just about what you eat, it is also about what you consume emotionally, mentally, and spiritually." ~Shamala Tan
"The trophy is earned in the hours when no one is watching." ~Unknown	"Energy flows where attention goes." ~Unknown	"Take care of your body; it's the only place you have to live." ~Jim Rohn

HEALTH
and
BEAUTY

Since this book is designed to reduce the stress and overwhelm of being a newly single woman, in this section I have included subjects directly related to your physical health and some basic beauty topics that may be relevant for you as a Newly Single Woman. Although you might argue that feeling pretty has nothing to do with health, I believe that when you feel pretty, your confidence goes up and stress and fear are reduced. This increased confidence supports you in taking action and trying new things which leads to your growth, which leads to your happiness, which supports your total wellness.

Back in 1948, The World Health Organization (WHO) recognized and stated that "Health is a resource for everyday life, not the objective of living."

That statement is such a great reminder that your health is a powerful asset for you in creating a life you love. When I refer to health, I refer to it with a holistic view. As we already discussed in the Happy Section, your body is fully connected with your mind and soul. For example, diet and exercise obviously affects the look and feel of your body. It also affects how the physical part of your brain functions and the way you think and feel emotionally. Coming out of a relationship or divorce can leave you drained, stressed, out of shape, exhausted, overwhelmed, uncertain, scared, or angry but it can also give you a sense of relief to have that phase of your life finalized. You can take back control over your own ways of being and how you will show up in your new life. You have the power to create new routines and habits that work for you to improve your wellbeing and confidence. Let your beauty from within shine outward as you radiate good health!

Water

You have probably heard to drink eight 8oz glasses of water daily. That is actually a minimum. Many experts now recommend ten to fifteen glasses a day for women. (If you are being more active and/or sweating heavily, or are pregnant, the amount needed goes up even more).

Water is the one thing you need to survive as a human. Your body can survive remarkably for weeks without food but without water for a day, your body will begin to malfunction. Water is in all of your cells and is needed for almost every task that your body performs.

- Blood circulation
- Breathing
- Metabolism and absorption of nutrients
- Regulation of body temperature
- Waste removal and detoxification
- Reduces wrinkles by keeping the cells full and plump and skin healthy.

Experts agree that to maintain your wellbeing you need to drink water regularly every day. I find it a good practice to drink my first 8-16 oz. early in my day, soon after I wake up. This way your body can start the day hydrated and ready to support your activities. It also gives your body time to process the water and pee before you head out the door so you do not get caught needing a restroom before you get where you are going!

If drinking 8-15 glasses of water daily seems difficult to you, the good news is that even coffee, tea, or juice can count toward your water intake totals– but drink regular water too (and avoid sodas because they can dehydrate you and leach density from your bones over time). There are also ways to add flavor to your water to make it more flavorful. Drop a few bits of natural flavor into your water with pieces of lemons, limes, oranges, cucumbers, blueberries, strawberries, cherries, etc. Many bottled water brands have already done this for you with water flavors that entice you to drink more. These are great options but do not get caught up in the waters with sweeteners (or worse, artificial sweeteners) in them. Water is all natural and should stay that way!

Sleep

How are you sleeping at night? Sleep is so important for you to feel well and to have the energy to do all the fantastic things calling out to you! The standard healthy average is about 8 hours per night but some may need more and some less. Your sleep needs can also change based on the circumstances in your life since stress, excitement, sadness, physical activity, diet, and/or illness will affect the amounts of sleep you need over time.

It is during sleep that your body can work on healing itself by balancing hormones, strengthening your immune system, and sorting and storing information in your brain. You know that when you do not get enough sleep you can feel tired, irritated, and have a hard time staying focused. A lack of sleep on a consistent basis can also put you at risk for serious medical conditions like heart disease, diabetes, anxiety, and depression.

Since sleep is so important to your total wellbeing, and so many people have sleep issues either falling asleep or staying asleep, I have included a few tips on how you can have quality sleep regularly.

- Go to sleep and wake up at the same time each day, even on the weekends. This helps to regulate your body's clock to help you to fall asleep and stay asleep throughout the night.

- Create and follow a relaxing bedtime ritual you follow each night. Even if it is simply showering, completing your skin care routine, reading a book, meditating or stretching. When done routinely, the ritual will signal to your brain that it is time to get ready for sleep.

- Exercise daily. Any exercise is better than no exercise, and at any time of day. I even found that although many people do not prefer to exercise right before bed, for me, even just walking on my treadmill 15 minutes before bed can help me to fall asleep easier.

- Avoid naps, especially in the afternoon. Although you may need a nap occasionally because of certain situations, don't create a nap habit since that can also affect your body's clock and can disrupt your sleep at nighttime.

- Avoid caffeine, cigarettes, and alcohol since these can all disrupt your sleep.

- Avoid heavy or spicy meals right before bed. It can be uncomfortable to try to sleep with a full stomach so eat meals at least a few hours before bedtime.

- Avoid bright lights, and digital electronics right before bed. If you need to be on your phone or tablet, look for the nighttime mode to enable a more restful dimmer light and reduce the blue light effects. Studies show that the standard light emanating from our electronics actually stimulates our brain which can make it harder for you to fall asleep.

Special note: Eyeglass lenses are now being manufactured with filters built in that reduce the harmful effects of blue light from electronics. Check for them anywhere that sells prescription glasses.

- Stay off social media right before bed since the content on the feeds can cause excitement, stress or anxiety which can make it difficult to fall asleep or remain asleep.

- If you can't get to sleep, don't just lay in bed for hours, go into another room and do something until you feel tired, then go back to your bed.

- Another strategy to calm your mind is to direct your thoughts to something positive. I like making a mental list of all my blessings. This helps me fall asleep in a state of gratitude which is a wonderful state to be in.

Food

To support your body it is important to provide the necessary ingredients for your systems to function properly. Your food is obviously important to your mental and physical wellbeing. Today, there are so many amazing options to help you eat a diet that is healthy and has a wide variety of flavors and textures. Dieticians suggest that we include as much <u>natural</u> color in our diet as possible. This means lots of vegetables and fruits. When you go grocery shopping think about how much color you can eat with each meal or on each day or week. I found there are easy ways to include more veggies even in our "normal" meals by grating or dicing the vegetables before adding them.

For example, one meal I love to cook is chili which can already be very healthy with beans, tomatoes, and proteins. When my girls were little, I also began to grate up zucchini and include these small pieces in the chili. Very few people even noticed and they eat the powerful nutrients in each delicious bite!

If you have the time, money, and talent to cook from fresh, organic foods at home, that is wonderful! To create excitement, you may want to try new recipes, get away from your old standards and ensure that you build in as much variety as possible. Maybe designate one night a week to try something totally new! Or try to update a recipe you have loved for years to incorporate new flavors!

Another way to enjoy new tastes is to explore foods from different cultures. I used to tell my kids that since I could not take them to every country at least they could explore a bit of different cultures through foods. Food is always a central aspect of every culture. You can go to specialty restaurants and shops, explore new cookbooks or recipes online, and even buy foods at specialty grocery shops or online from all around the globe! Experiment with new foods and have fun! Whatever lifestyle you live, find ways to ensure you are getting the nutrients you need to fuel your body, mind, and spirit.

Here are a few other strategies to help work healthy meals into your life and busy schedule.

Frozen Foods

If you do not enjoy cooking, or simply need a faster meal option, consider frozen foods. There are now many healthy frozen options. Remember the same rule – look for natural ingredients (organic and non-GMO are best), and a variety of natural colors and textures in each meal.

Fast Food or Quick Serve Restaurants

If you must pick up something quick try to keep it light. Here are some basic guidelines:

- Pick menu options that are not breaded.
- Choose grilled or baked and avoid fried foods.

- Order salads or fresh foods when possible.

- Avoid lots of sauces.

- Avoid sodas.

Delivered Meal Kit Services

There are many meal service options that will deliver your prepped meals to your home. Then you just spend a few moments cooking the ingredients each night for fresh and healthy meals.

I have listed a few of the larger companies below with a quote from their website. These companies may also offer different menu options: paleo, vegetarian, vegan, gluten-free, organic, etc.

- Sunbasket.com – "Organic and sustainable ingredients & delicious recipes delivered weekly. Paleo, lean & clean, gluten-free, vegetarian, and family options."

- Blue Apron.com – "Blue Apron's uniquely integrated model means better ingredients, better pricing and a better planet for us all."

- Hello Fresh – "We Shop, Plan, and Deliver step-by-step recipes and ingredients so you can just relax and enjoy all there is to love about cooking. And eating."

- HomeChef.com – "Home Cooking Made Simple

- Home Chef delivers everything you need to bring more delicious meals and moments to the table. Every day."

Specialty Restaurants

Vegetarian and vegan restaurants are also popping up in many cities. Since there are so many new foods and ingredients available from all over the world, chefs have been able to create delicious culinary delights with no animal byproducts.

I highly recommend trying these types of places if you are so inclined. Go into the experience with an adventurous attitude. If you order something that sounds familiar, say pizza or "chicken" teriyaki, do not expect them to be exactly like the foods you are accustomed to. They will be great in their own right but they will not be exactly like what the name may conjure up in your mind.

Special note: If this is your first foray into trying vegan foods, order a few things to try. Stay away from ordering dishes that have the main ingredient as "cheese" for your only entrée on your first visit. Although vegan cheese can be delicious it differs greatly from dairy cheese.

Also, many vegan foods can contain nuts so be careful if you have any food allergies. Always ask the restaurant staff for more information if you want to know what is in their recipes. They are likely quite familiar with answering questions about ingredients for people.

Some vegan chains that have been expanding and may now be found in your city are listed below with a blurb from their website:

- Veggie Grill is a fast food restaurant that sells 100% yummy vegan food.
  https://www.veggiegrill.com/

- Amy's Drive Thru is a fast food restaurant serving up organic, local, vegetarian, and non-GMO fare. http://www.amysdrivethru.com/

- Native Foods America's premier fast-casual vegan restaurant group spanning coast to coast.
  https://www.nativefoods.com/

- Vgë Café Pure Vegetarian. Healthier.
  Vegan Fast Casual Franchise
  http://www.vgecafefranchise.com/

Vitamin supplements

Another simple way to ensure your body has everything it needs is to take a high quality daily multi-vitamin/mineral supplement. You can add additional supplements based on your particular needs.

Research shows that taking supplements can greatly improve your health and life by managing your body's functions, reducing the effects of stress, depression, and anxiety while improving alertness, focus, happiness, energy levels, and general well-being.

There are many vitamins and minerals that our bodies need regularly, for this book I focused on several that are proven to help you cope with stress, and maintain a more positive mood.

As always, check with your doctor before taking anything new to see what is right for you. Every person's needs are different.

I am not a doctor and am not prescribing any specific diet for the readers of this book. This information is intended to inform and empower you to validate and implement what is best for you and your unique self.

The B Complex Vitamins

There are eight B vitamins and they are all especially important for dealing with stress, maintaining energy levels by assisting in the breakdown of foods, keeping your blood healthy, preventing memory loss, slowing the signs of aging, improving your mood and preventing depression.

The B complex vitamins are also critically important for pregnant women because they are needed for normal growth and development of the baby.

Low levels of the B Vitamins may leave you feeling easily stressed, unfocused, tired, anxious or depressed. Other common affects you may experience with Vitamin B deficiency are: digestive issues, skin issues, and muscle weakness and/or pain.

Food sources that provide the different B Vitamins:

Vitamin	Name	Food Source
Vitamin B1	Thiamine	whole grains, meat, fish, legumes, seeds, nuts
Vitamin B2	Riboflavin	eggs, meat, organ meats, milk, green vegetables
Vitamin B3	Niacin	meat, fish, poultry, mushrooms, peanuts
Vitamin B5	Pantothenic acid	meat, dairy, eggs, legumes, mushrooms, avocados, broccoli, sweet potatoes
Vitamin B6	Pyridoxine	poultry, fish (especially Yellow fin tuna and Salmon), organ meats, potatoes, starchy vegetables, non-citrus fruits, and fortified breakfast cereals.
Vitamin B7	Biotin	meat, fish, poultry, eggs, dairy.
Vitamin B9	Folate or Folic acid	green leafy vegetables, liver, yeast, black-eyed peas, Brussels sprouts
Vitamin B12	Cobalamin	fish (especially Rainbow Trout and Salmon), clams, liver, animal foods of all kinds, nori (seaweed), cheese.

Special Note: Vitamin B12 and B9 (Folic Acid):
Some people do not easily absorb and process folate (B9) and vitamin B12 and need Vitamin B Complex injections. These shots allow your body to metabolize the Vitamin B differently and more readily absorb the nutrients. You can get them at many vitamin shops, medical spas, or doctors' offices.

As always, check with your doctor before taking anything new to see what is right for you. Every person's needs are different.

Vitamin C:

Vitamin C may be the most widely known vitamin for helping to eliminate your cold and flu symptoms, but did you know it also reduces risks and symptoms of heart disease, cancer, diabetes, and Alzheimer's and is even known for promoting firm youthful looking skin (you can find it in many skin products). On top of all that vitamin C is important for its positive effects on mood, brain function and the reduction of stress. It helps your body to synthesize serotonin so you can stay happier and less stressed.

Food Sources of Vitamin C: Citrus fruits (and juices), strawberries, cherries, pineapple, papaya, guava, kiwi, melons, peppers, tomatoes, cilantro, thyme, parsley, broccoli, Brussels sprouts, cauliflower, and kale.

Calcium:

Calcium is the most common mineral found throughout your body and it is another important nutrient to avoid depression and boost your mood. You often see calcium paired with vitamin D (think dairy milk) because Vitamin D is also needed for the mineral to be absorbed into your body through your intestines.

Calcium is required for the formation of bones and teeth. It is necessary for muscle contractions, blood clotting, the release of hormones and enzymes, and the transmission of messages from the brain through the nerves to every part of your body.

Low levels of calcium can lead to muscle cramps and spasms, numbness and tingling in the hands, feet, and face, depression, brittle nails, weakened bones, and osteoporosis.

Food sources of Calcium: milk, yogurt, cheese, fruits like oranges and kiwi, seafood, legumes, broccoli, and leafy greens like kale or bok choy.

Vitamin D

Vitamin D is important in regulating your moods and since it helps your body absorb Calcium, it keeps your bones healthy. Vitamin D also helps alleviate symptoms of depression, regulate your immune system, and might help fight heart disease and multiple types of cancer.

Low levels of vitamin D have been linked to numerous diseases including many types of cancer, heart disease, diabetes, Alzheimer's, Parkinson's, depression, chronic fatigue syndrome and more.

It is estimated that over half of Americans and people all over the world, are deficient in Vitamin D. People more at risk for deficiency are:

- People that do not eat dairy.

- Vegans and Vegetarians since most natural Vitamin D food sources are animal based.

- People who do not get in the sun often.

- People with dark skin because the darker pigment reduces the body's conversion of sunlight to Vitamin D.

- Older people because the body slows production as we age.

- People who have kidney problems since kidneys are critical in the conversion of sunlight to Vitamin D in your body.

- People who are obese. Although doctors still are unsure why, they are in agreement that obese people have lower levels of Vitamin D.

- People that have any intestinal problems which would reduce the body's capacity to absorb Vitamin D directly.

Food sources of Vitamin D: fortified dairy products, cereals, and orange juice, egg, fish (especially salmon and swordfish), mushrooms.

You can also get your daily dose of Vitamin D from exposure to moderate sunlight every day (amounts needed vary by person and be careful not to overexpose and burn).

Magnesium

Magnesium is needed for your body to maintain healthy bones, heart muscles, and nerves. It plays a part in over 600 metabolic functions in the body. Magnesium is very helpful in managing stress, keeping you calm and helping you to relax which also helps you to sleep better. It also helps to develop serotonin (one of our happy chemicals) to increase your feelings of happiness.

Estimates say that 70-80% of the U.S. population is deficient in Magnesium. When magnesium is low, anxiety, irritability, insomnia, and fatigue will increase and you will have trouble relaxing.

Food sources of Magnesium: almonds, cashews, peanuts, edamame/soy products, whole grain bread and cereal, black beans, avocado, spinach. Magnesium is a mineral which can also be found in mineral waters such as Perrier, and Evian brands.

Zinc

Zinc is found within all of your body tissues and is needed for healthy cell division, hormone balance, ability to cope with stress, and it helps to slow the aging process. It plays a role in the production of our happy chemical serotonin, your ability to heal wounds, aids digestion, prevents diarrhea, and helps with overall immune function.

When Zinc is taken at the first sign of illness (a bit of cough or sniffle), it can help to lessen the severity of the cold symptoms and shorten the length of the illness.

Low levels of zinc can lead to increased stress, anxiety, and depression, a weakened immune system, poor concentration, dementia, memory loss, hair loss, anemia, and learning disabilities.

Food sources of Zinc: oysters, crab or lobster, and animal products such as meats and dairy. Although Zinc is present in some plant-based foods, the body does not readily absorb it from these forms. Because of this reduced absorption, vegetarians may need to take more zinc than non-vegetarians to get the amounts they need.

As always, check with your doctor before taking anything new to see what is right for you. Every person's needs are different.

Probiotics

Probiotics are the good type of bacteria that line your digestive tract. They are critical to your body's ability to absorb the nutrients you give it for optimizing all areas of your health. Probiotics have been proven to prevent/treat urinary tract infections, help heal leaky gut syndrome, increase energy levels, reduce occurrences of colds and flu, and promote beautiful skin.

Low levels of probiotics can produce digestive disorders, skin issues, and frequent colds and flu.

Food sources of Probiotics: yogurt, kefir (dairy or coconut based), apple cider vinegar, kombucha, fermented vegetables (like sauerkraut, kimchi and even miso), high-quality soluble fermentable fiber (chia seeds, flaxseeds, organic fruits, and vegetables).

Exercise

As your lifestyle and situation have changed, you may have more or less time to yourself and you may have more or less money to yourself, but there are many ways to fit exercise into your life.

Regular exercise will increase your health, vitality and positive feelings, confidence, and levels of happiness. It also increases your energy levels by increasing your metabolism. This is awesome since you will want the energy to put towards your new life and activities.

Special note: Clear everything with your doctor before you start any new routine or if you have any questions or concerns. Also, remember, if you have never done strength and/or cardio workouts before that your muscles will hurt a day or two later but this normal, it is just a reminder to yourself that you have done something good for your body and that you are strong and getting stronger! If you are uncertain about any pain or discomfort you feel, contact your doctor for an evaluation.

Ideas to fit exercise into your day:

- Walking, hiking, jogging, running
- Riding a bike, skateboard, scooter
- Dancing
- Yoga
- Jumping on a trampoline, jumping rope
- Swimming/hydro exercises
- Skiing, snowboarding
- Golfing – on course or at the driving range
- Weight lifting, Circuit training
- Climbing stairs
- Gardening
- Team sports - with a league, family, or friends

To maximize your time throughout the day, you can even play little games with your small chunks of time. Have fun filling your little bits of time with some bursts of intensity. This helps to keep your energy up and add to your exercise success. For example, when you put something in the microwave, instead of just standing around waiting for the minutes to go by, do squats or leg lifts, or dance around the kitchen until the bell chimes. While you are waiting at an airport, you can walk up and down the terminals to get a power walk in instead of heading to sit at the gate, a restaurant, or bar. When my daughters were little I would wait in the bathroom stall with them and I would do wall squats while they did their business on the toilet. I have also done wall squats during elevator rides. The point is that these little minutes throughout the day can become fun and productive little inspirations for you!

Many people feel like there just isn't enough time in their week to fit in a regular exercise routine. I have felt like this at different times in my life too. When you break it down though, it may blow your mind to realize you may have more time than you think! Think about this: there are 24 hours in a day and 7 days a week, that equals to 168 hours per week. Say you sleep 8 hours every night; you still have 112 hours left each week. Ok, let's subtract 50 hours a week for work if you have a full time job, and you still have 62 hours remaining each week. Now, let's say you spend 35 hours a week (5 hours per day) commuting, running errands, spending time with family and friends. That still leaves 27 hours available of open time per week! Isn't that incredible? The first time I did the math on this, I was shocked. The natural response you may have to this is, "What is happening with this unaccounted for time?" With 27 hours of free time each week, you can prioritize at least 30 minutes a day (3.5 hours/week) to exercise. Any consistent exercise routine will reap rewards with your body, mind, and spirit. It feels so great to be healthy and strong and feel beautiful!

Fitness Blogs and Websites

Having positive resources in your life to engage with allow you to be a part of healthy communities (like newlysinglewomencommunity.com) that can broaden your outlook and provide ideas that spark your enthusiasm to try something new, whether it be a new exercise, a recipe, new friendships, or even new perspectives. Here are a few health and fitness blogs that have powerful content and can be great resources for information for you as a Newly Single Woman.

As always, check with your doctor before taking on anything new to see what is right for you. Every person's needs are different.

- *Healthline:* Stated mission is to be your most trusted ally in your pursuit of health and well-being. https://www.healthline.com

- *American Council on Exercise (ACE):* Stated mission is to share science-backed training and information to U.S. fitness professionals and the general public. https://www.acefitness.org/education-and-resources/professional/expert-articles?

- *Life by Daily Burn, Fitness Daily Burn:* Stated mission is to be a subscription-based app and website offering exercise programs. There are step-by-step workouts with videos and advice for overall health and wellness on this site. http://dailyburn.com/life/category/fitness/

- **_Breaking Muscle:_** (multiple authors) Stated mission is to be a site written by people who are passionate about health and want to share information with people at all fitness levels. https://breakingmuscle.com/

- **_POPSUGAR Fitness:_** Stated mission: A global media and technology company, Popsugar publishes digital content across many topics and also offers many fitness articles and videos with a fun, edgy attitude. https://www.popsugar.com/fitness/

Special Note: There are many resources available for health and fitness. The list of websites included here is just a sample of what was available at the time I wrote this book. You can search on any keyword to find additional resources and/or information.

Streaming Exercise Videos and Exercise Apps

These workout sources are great because they are available anytime from anywhere to maximize your time. Many blogs and/or websites, including some of the ones listed above, will have exercise videos you can download and/or stream to build a fitness routine that meets your needs. Another big fitness community, Beachbody.com has products and services and video on demand for you to select the best fits for your preferences and fitness goals.

Fitness apps are another great option for exercise routines and/or 30/60/90-day challenges that increase difficulty levels over time and track your progress. The best way to find these is to go to the app store on your smartphone or tablet and search for 'Fitness' or 'Fitness Challenges' or put in a specific body part that you want to work on, like: 'abs', 'arms' 'thigh' or 'butt'. This will bring up the options for you and you can scroll through to find the ones that are the best fit for you.

As always, check with your doctor before taking on anything new to see what is right for you. Every person's needs are different.

In-Home Exercise Equipment

OK, so for me this is where I had a big fitness breakthrough. Going through my divorce and all the stress and sadness left me out of shape and mentally and emotionally tired. Being a single Mom also left me with little time to leave the house alone to walk or run outside or to go to the gym since I could not leave my children alone when they were younger.

Looking for solutions, I decided that what I needed was something I could do at the house anytime day or night, and something where I did not need to concentrate or think about what I was doing (like exercise routines) since I may be doing it while I was very tired. I wanted something I could do for my body and just clear my mind. For me, the solution was buying a treadmill. It was an investment of several hundred dollars and I had to determine where I would put it in the house, but I have always been happy with my purchase. I would get on the treadmill after the kids went to bed and jog-walk for miles. Before I knew it I had changed my body and was in better shape than I had been in years. I was also feeling much better about myself and my body. From there I added exercise weight routines and started all sorts of new activities (like hiking, biking, kayaking, paddle boarding, swimming, camping, etc.) which brought such a sense of pride and excitement to my life.

If you think in-home equipment is something that you want, ensure you think about what you would most enjoy and what would be something you would use consistently before you buy. There are many types of equipment you can buy for your home, so review your options before you purchase anything.

Special note: Before purchasing any exercise equipment check for weight limits and adjustable features to ensure it is safe for you and will fit your body. Although the foldable or stow-able equipment might sound more suitable, any equipment you can keep out and ready for use makes it more simple and a great reminder for you to do use it regularly. If you can just jump on when you are ready rather than having to pull it out and set it up, you will use it more often.

As always, check with your doctor before taking on anything new to see what is right for you. Every person's needs are different.

Here are some of the major categories of equipment available:

Treadmills

These are like "moving sidewalks" and are great for you to walk, jog, or run while in your home environment.

These basic features are recommended in a treadmill: Electronic controls for speed, incline, and distance, time, and a fan with multiple speeds. It should also indicate the calories burned and heart rate.

Additional features that also can make your workout more enjoyable are MP3 hookups, a TV screen, pre-programmed workout routines, and the ability to fold and store away when not in use.

Treadmill Alternatives:

There are different types of machines in this category but they are designed to be easier on the joints. Some can actually even outperform treadmills in calorie burn. Many have features that provide versatility so you can switch up your routine as needed.

These basic features are recommended in a treadmill alternative machine: Electronic controls for speed, incline, distance, time, and a fan with multiple speeds. It should also indicate the calories burned and heart rate. (Features will depend on the type of machine you get and there may be others that are not listed here.)

Additional features that also can make your workout more enjoyable are MP3 hookups, cup holder, a TV screen, pre-programmed workout routines.

Stationary Bikes:

For those that love to ride bikes or that want a great cardio solution easier on the joints – great for recovery of knee injuries too. The bicycle is the machine offered in the most shapes and sizes. There are small models, models that fold away, and high-tech bikes connected to live classes happening in NYC (onePeloton.com).

Special note: If you choose a bike, I recommend getting the most complete bike that your budget and space can accommodate. Since you sit on the bike, it is critical that you can position your body comfortably and that the machine can be adjusted to fit your size. Having a seat that is adjustable up and down and front and back is necessary for shorter women. When in use, the top of the seat should be positioned in line with your hipbone when you stand upright next to the bike. When seated, your leg should be extended with a slight bend (about 25-35 degree) at the knee. When you pedal, the balls of your feet should be on the pedal.

These basic features are recommended in a stationary bike: Electronic controls for speed, resistance, distance, time, a fan with multiple speeds and tracking of your calories burned and heart rate. The bike seat is important so you are comfortable while you ride. You can get a bike with a wider seat and/or you can buy a "saddle pad" that covers the seat with more cushion (available on Amazon and many other stores).

Additional features that also can make your workout more enjoyable are MP3 hookups, cup holder, a TV screen, pre-programmed workout routines or connections to real-time classes.

Elliptical Machine/Elliptical Trainer

Stationary exercise machines where the user puts each foot onto a small platform and pushes each in a smooth flow alternating between legs. The platform moves forward and around in an elliptical shape. This burns calories while being easy on the joints.

These basic features are recommended in an elliptical machine: Electronic controls for speed, resistance, ramp control/incline, distance, time, and a fan with multiple speeds. It should also indicate the calories burned and heart rate.

Additional features that also can make your workout more enjoyable are MP3 hookups, cup holder, a TV screen, pre-programmed workout routines.

Home Gyms

Exercise machines that contain multiple parts with weights, tension, bars, and pulleys designed so the user can perform lots of different exercises to strengthen different parts of their body. These gyms are generally compact and designed to fit in the home. You should be able to easily understand how to perform the various exercises on the device so you can use the equipment safely.

You can purchase home gym systems by brands like Bowflex®, Gold's Gym, or Powerline, etc.

Free Weights, Dumbbells, Cowbells, Balls, and Bands

These pieces of equipment are easy to use and don't take up a lot of space in your home. You can find a selection at Amazon, Target, Walmart, and most sporting goods stores. Adding these tools to your workouts can help you to get in shape faster and build more muscle (which increases your metabolism). Start with lower weights and more repetitions to build lean muscle.

Special note: You must be careful to stay in proper form when using any free weight equipment so you do not hurt yourself. Get instructions for the specific equipment you buy and talk with your doctor before starting any new exercise routine.

The Gym (outside the home)

Ok, those two words will stir some sort of emotion in you. They could evoke a sense of excitement or maybe a sense of apprehension for you. There is no need to dread the gym because today there are many gym options available to you that can be fun and productive.

Think about what kind of environment you would look forward to being in each week. If you feel good while you are there, and look forward to going, you will go more often, get more exercise, and get the most value from your membership.

Other things to consider when looking for the right gym for you are:

- Do the hours they are open work for your schedule?

- Do they have quality, safe equipment available to you?

- Do the machines adjust to fit your body (some do not adjust enough for petite women to use them properly)?

- Do they have the amenities you need/want: pools, courts, classes, etc.?

- Do they have classes that interest you? (Yoga, circuit training, Zumba, etc.) Do the class schedules work with your schedule?

- Do they have physical trainers available to answer your questions?

- Is it close to your house or work? Can you go to other locations with your membership? How many locations do they have and where?

Personal Physical Trainers

A personal physical trainer can be an effective way to build accountability and ensure you are getting your exercise consistently. A good trainer will work with you to customize your workout to reach the fitness and/or body shape objectives you have for yourself. They will add variety to your workouts so you don't get bored or go easy on yourself, and ensure you are doing effective workouts with good form to push you and to reach your objectives.

Body Therapies

I listed these things together here because they are all excellent ways to assist your body, mind, and spirit to balance and heal. You may have heard of some of these and may have not. As we talked about earlier, you must take a holistic approach to your wellbeing. Being healthy, feeling good, and looking good, all work together: Mind. Body. Spirit.

Each of the following methods works with your body and the energy within to bring you back into a state of balance. If you are interested in trying any of the following methods, I suggest you ask your friends for references or search for and read the reviews of the locations near you before you book an appointment.

I have used these treatments at different times throughout my life and have found each one helpful. I share them with you here to expand your perspective on what is available to you and to explore options that you can evaluate for your own needs and life.

Special note: As always, check with your doctor before taking on anything new to see what is right for you. Every person's needs are different.

Since many western doctors may not "believe" in these treatments, the key here if you want to try them, is not whether your doctor believes they "will work" but to ensure your doctor does not think they would be harmful to you. Do not do anything that your doctor does not clear you for. Additionally, be sure to tell your selected practitioner(s) about any medical issues you have so they are aware and can take a holistic approach to current situations and your overall well-being.

Ensure that you feel comfortable with any practitioner(s) that you select, and that they take time to listen to you and respect your questions and requests. Because they will be working with the energy in your body, some types of treatments will touch our body and others may not. They can all have positive benefits on your energetic, physical, mental, and spiritual parts.

Special note: Do not worry if they ask to see your tongue. Many good practitioners in these doctrines can gain strong insights into your health from the look, color, and texture of your tongue.

Massage

A massage therapist uses their hands, fingers, elbows, knees, forearm, feet, or a device, to rub, knead, pat, stroke, or tap your skin and muscles.

This results in improved circulation, increased suppleness, and relief from tension and pain. It can also be effective for reducing symptoms of disorders associated with the muscles, joints, and the nervous system.

Acupuncture

The ancient Chinese practice of inserting fine needles into specific points of your body (called Chakras) to affect the energy flow within your whole being.

Acupuncture needles do not look anything like the medical needles used to draw blood or administer shots.

They are even thinner than a sewing needle or stick pin since there is no need for any fluid to flow through it.

Acupuncture is most commonly used to reduce chronic pain such as: arthritic pain, headaches, or pain in the back, neck, and knee. It is also known to provide relief for conditions like nausea, anxiety, insomnia, and depression, and even to help stop cravings.

Special note: If you have questions about your health, consult your doctor before trying anything new.

Side effects of acupuncture are rare but infection is possible at the site of the needles if handled with poor hygiene or untrained practitioners. Always ensure that the environment is clean and make sure that your practitioner uses only new needles for you. Since needles are packaged separately they should be opened at the time of use during your treatment session so ask them to see the needles before starting treatment.

Acupressure

Similar to acupuncture but without the needles. This therapy uses physical pressure applied with fingers, hands, elbows, or other means to the same points on the body used in acupuncture to clear energetic blockages and enable the free flow of energy.

It is used to relieve tension and/or pain and to promote healing. It may also be effective to help reduce fatigue and manage conditions like nausea, vomiting, stomach aches, and anxiety.

Special Note: If you have questions about your health, consult your doctor before trying anything new.

Cupping

This ancient Chinese therapy uses glass or plastic "cups" to draw blood flow to the skin to help relieve pain, and eliminate the toxins that have been stored in the tissues of your body. The objective of a cupping treatment is to rebalance the flow of your energy by improving the condition of you blood and lymph tissues.

The practitioner will use heat or a hand instrument to suction different size "cups" onto the skin. Where the "cup" attaches, the skin inside becomes raised as it is sucked up partway into the "cup." You will remain with the "cups" attached to your skin for a few minutes while you relax. (My daughter thinks this part of the treatment feels good). After the practitioner removes the "cups" with a little pop sound, you may see cup shaped bruises on the treated areas. The bruises might last for several days to a week depending on the person.

Cupping can improve pain, inflammation, blood flow, relaxation and respiratory diseases such as the common cold, pneumonia, and bronchitis.

Special Note: Cupping is NOT to be used by patients who bleed easily and/or cannot stop bleeding, have skin ulcers, or retain excess fluids in the skin (edema). Pregnant women should seek approval from their doctors prior to any treatment but should never have their abdomen or lower back cupped.

If you have questions about your health, consult your doctor before trying anything new.

Pranic Healing

Pranic Healing is a form of energy medicine where your life energy "prana" is manipulated by the practitioner to heal ailments or disorders, and support overall mental and emotional well-being.

Since everything around us consists of energy, the practitioner can move, blend, cleanse, or add to the energy in your energetic field without even touching you. Their hands may linger or move just above your skin. This process treats your "energy body" which then improves your "physical body".

Pranic Healing is used to speed recovery after surgery, relieve migraines, reduce symptoms of diabetes, sinusitis, asthma, back pain, high blood pressure and arthritis.

Minor side effects from Pranic Healing sessions can include temporary headaches, and/or tiredness.

Special Note: If you have questions about your health, consult your doctor before trying anything new.

Reiki

A Japanese healing technique where the practitioner touches you with their hands to move, enhance, and balance the energy within the seven major chakras of your body. By doing this the practitioner can stimulate your own natural healing power from within.

Reiki is used to remove pain and heal physical wounds, infections, and inflammation. It also helps to manage sleep, sadness, stress, and negativity, depression, anxiety and support overall mental and emotional well-being.

Reiki also has been reported as helpful in treating some symptoms in cancer patients, such as depression, pain, and fatigue.

Temporary side effects possible after a Reiki session, are: upset stomach, indigestion, diarrhea or headaches, crying for unknown reasons, fatigue, feeling hot, cold or tingly, and increased urination. These effects are believed to result from the release of toxins or stored/blocked energy from your body during the session.

Special Note: If you have questions about your health, consult your doctor before trying anything new.

Chiropractors

So common they seem mainstream, Chiropractic medicine is still considered a form of alternative medicine. Interestingly it does not stem from Ancient Asia, like many of the other body treatments. Chiropractic therapy began in 1895, in the state of Iowa, U.S.A. and today is the number one alternative medicine therapy used in America.

Like the other body therapies above, chiropractic treatment does not include drugs or surgery. Practitioners evaluate, manipulate, and treat the spine with manual adjustments. This can be done by using the hands or assisted by an instrument to apply pressure to the affected joint area to restore mobility and alleviate pain. This helps the body to heal by ensuring the spine, and nerves stemming from it, are aligned correctly to help the whole body function properly.

Chiropractic therapy is mainly used to improve back pain, neck pain, arthritis/joint pain, scoliosis, headaches, bowel regularity, improved mental clarity, and ear infections.

Side effects from Chiropractic treatments can include temporary headaches, dizziness, tiredness, and/or discomfort in the parts of the body treated.

Special Note: If you have questions about your health, consult your doctor before trying anything new.

Skin Care

Your skin changes as you get older, so it is important to update your skin care to meet your skin's changing needs over the course of your life.

Having a skin care routine for your mornings and evening is important to help your skin look its absolute best. The routine must include at minimum a cleansing step and a moisturizing/hydrating step. There are also toners and specialty products you can layer into your routine if desired to promote faster or increased results. What you choose depends on your skin type, your skin needs, and your budget.

I must stop here and say that above all else:
USE SUNSCREEN DAILY!

Make sure it is labeled as broad spectrum, which means it will shield against UVA and UVB rays. There are two types available: chemical based or physical sunscreen formulations. The physical barriers are made up of titanium dioxide and/or zinc oxide. Remember the white cream used on noses at the beach? That is the zinc oxide ingredient but today's lotions use it in a much lighter formulation to achieve the same great blocking benefits. These physical formulations may feel a bit heavier than the chemical formulations but they are less likely to cause skin irritations or allergies.(Most baby sunscreens are of this variety).

The chemical formulations can feel much lighter. Because they absorb into the skin better, they are easier to wear underneath makeup.

Doctors recommend an SPF between 30-50 SPF be applied to your face every day (That is above and beyond any sunscreen in your foundation makeup.) I have taught my daughters to put at least a 30 SPF on their face Every. Single. Day. (I use 50-100 SPF).

Even if you plan to be inside all day, still apply sunscreen to your face. It is the habit that is important. This is a critical part of your morning routine. Even on a cloudy day your skin can get burned from the sun's rays.

Although the face coverage is a must every day, the other parts of the body can be optional depending on what you are doing and how much of your time will be outdoors. Remember that if you drive or ride in a car a lot or are going on road trips that your arms may still get a lot of sun (coming from the car windows) and they will need to be protected. As a woman, you will also want to maintain a beautiful décolletage area throughout your life and so be diligent in wearing sunscreen on your chest and shoulders also when out if these parts are exposed.

Shade

Since most wrinkles are caused by sun damage, some of the best prevention techniques are to block the sun entirely with sunglasses and hats, or umbrellas when you are outside in the sunshine.

The bigger the glasses and bigger the hat, the more effective they will be because they will cover more of your face. Your sunglasses should be UV-coated to protect your vision by preventing the UV rays from penetrating the internal parts of your eyes, and can also protect the fragile skin around your eyes. They will lessen your need to squint too since they will reduce the brightness and glare from the sun and this also helps to prevent wrinkles.

A hat offers many of the same benefits as sunglasses but also shades your head. Have you ever gotten a sun-burn on the strip of skin showing in the part of your hair? The hat will protect your head, face, neck, and ears from sunburn while you are out. A hat with a 4" rim or more is recommended to provide the best shading. Although many of us wear hats at the pool or beach, it is a good idea to wear them whenever out for an extended period of time outdoors (but still use sunscreen as well).

You can also find hats and clothing with a UV coating already on them to protect the skin further from the rays that may penetrate the fabric fibers of untreated garments. You can search the internet for "clothing with sunscreen" and you will find many results to shop through. There is also a product you can wash into your clothes call Rit Sun Guard. You add it to the wash cycle of your laundry and it adds an SPF 30 protection that lasts on your garments for about 20 wears.

Posture

Whether you are sleeping or sitting, where you rest your head can impact the development of wrinkles over time. The best position to sleep in is on your back so you have gravity working in your favor to pull the skin back vs pressuring your face into a pillow.

If you hold your face in your hands a lot or rub your eyes consistently, you may unknowingly add wrinkles to your face. I had a friend that would regularly prop his face with a pen to the cheek and over the years wrinkles formed in the middle of his check exactly where he would position the pen. Also, if you are propping your chin in your hands this can smoosh the skin upward and over time develop wrinkles in those creases.

Air

Smoking is direct pollution into your lungs and skin. This will cause you to age faster from the inside and the outside. Your body and skin cells need clean oxygen to work their best. Inhaling smoke prevents you from getting the needed oxygen and important nutrients into your cells. It also damages the collagen fibers that keep your skin firm.

As discussed above, consistent behaviors can lead to wrinkles, so you will also create more wrinkles around your mouth if you regularly pucker your lips to inhale.

Exfoliation

Exfoliating your skin is an important part of your skin care routine especially as you get older. By effectively removing the dead skin cells, you can reveal smoother, clearer, more radiant looking skin while also allowing the skin cells to better absorb any other products you apply, making all of your efforts more effective.

There are two main types of exfoliants: physical or chemical. A physical exfoliator is a scrub with little bits of rough material that when rubbed onto the skin will physically buff away the impurities and dead skin cells. A chemical one will use either an acid or enzyme-based formula to dry the skin cells and cause them to flake and/or peel off revealing your new skin from underneath. The most common ingredients in a chemical formula are alpha-hydroxy acid (like glycolic acid) or a beta-hydroxy acid (like salicylic acid).

I use a combination of the two types of exfoliator formulations. For a few days, I may use a chemical based one to help remove old and reveal new skin cells but then use a physical scrub to remove any dead cells now lingering on my skin. I love the smooth feel I get from using the physical scrub products.

Special note: Every person's needs are different. I am not a doctor and am not prescribing any specific diet for the readers of this book. This information is intended to inform and empower you to validate and implement what is best for you and your unique self.

Before exfoliating, cleanse the area so you are not rubbing any makeup or dirt and germs into your skin. It is most commonly recommended to exfoliate your skin one to two times per week. Be careful not to do it too often because if you over-exfoliate it can cause skin irritation, inflammation, and increased oil production, which may lead to breakouts. (I learned this the hard way!)

Special note: Exfoliating can be done anywhere you have skin. It need not be limited to your face. Try exfoliating your throat and chest, elbows, feet, heals, and legs for smooth, soft skin. Exfoliating your legs before shaving can give you the smoothest surface for the razor to glide on, giving you a closer more perfect shave.

A cheap, natural exfoliator I use in the shower often is regular table salt! Just add a palmful of salt to a squirt of your body wash and rub anywhere. The result is silky smooth feeling skin! Voila!

Go Professional

Professional facials are a great way to keep your skin looking its best. They can improve your skin in ways that you cannot at home since they are experts in the latest treatments, have access to professional grade products, can use lights/lasers, are licensed to perform extractions, micro-dermabrasion, and administer *Botox*® and fillers.

Ensure that you always schedule your facials, or any professional skin treatment, with a trained, licensed dermatologist or aesthetician (person licensed to provide cosmetic skin care treatments and services). If you can afford it and can make the time, I recommend getting a professional facial every 30-60 days.

This section would not be complete without mentioning the benefits of seeing a dermatologist. Although most commonly known for curing acne and skin cancer, they can also prescribe creams, lotions, or oral medications that can help improve the look of your skin and slow the signs of aging.

One of the most effective treatments for the reduction and prevention of wrinkles (and acne) is the regular application of a Retin-A product. (Retin-A is actually a brand name and the generic form of the product with the same active ingredient is called Tretinoin). This is a prescription only ingredient. If used, remember that the Vitamin A compounds in the product can make your skin more sensitive to sunlight. Only use the crème at night and be even more careful about applying your sunscreen daily and using your protective gear like sunglasses and hats when using Retin-A products.

The treatments can also be very drying to the skin since the purpose is to slowly remove the top cells to reveal the healthy new ones underneath. Because of this, make sure you are using hydrating cleansers and moisturizers to balance the effects of the Retin-A and limit any other products that would be drying to your skin, like glycolic acid or benzoyl peroxide. Talk with your dermatologist about your total skin care plan.

Also, if you see an aesthetician for a facial while using any of these products, make sure you tell them about your routine since your skin can also be more sensitive to some of the treatments they may typically use and they may need to make adjustments for you.

Makeup

Many women create their makeup routine when they are young and keep it the same throughout their life. As you get older though, the colors, products and techniques used before may need to be updated. New ways of applying your makeup and new products that become available may help you look your best now.

Whether you want to minimize lines, banish blemishes, improve your lashes, or reduce redness, there are many products and application techniques that work great at every age. Here are a few tips and products I have found helpful in updating my routines to look my best as my skin and face change with time.

Primer

Makeup primer is a base step (like priming a wall before painting) that prepares your skin for the makeup foundation that follows. It allows the makeup to go on smoother and last longer. There are many types of primers. Those that reduce shine, even skin tones, hide imperfections, minimize pore size, moisturize the skin, provide sun protection, and fight aging. There are even primers that include ingredients to tighten your skin and create a facelift effect.

There are also specialty primers made specifically for lips and eyelids. It is great to prime your lips and the areas around your lips to keep your lipstick in place longer and to prevent lipstick from feathering into any wrinkles around the mouth. The eyelid primers can help prevent creasing, minimize eye wrinkles and keep eyeshadow and eyeliner in place longer.

Foundation/Base

There are many, many brands and varieties of foundation formulas out there to meet the needs of everyone. Here is basic guidance for selecting the best foundation option for you.

Special note: choose a color that matches your skin tone or one just slightly darker (don't go lighter). Make sure the color you use blends well with the skin tone of your neck so your face is not significantly lighter or darker than your neck and make sure you blend it all the way around your jawbone so there is no visible line near the edge of your face.

- **For Anti-aging effects and to soften lines**
  A cream foundation helps best to minimize lines. Anti-aging foundations restore moisture, stimulate collagen production, tighten skin, and reduce the appearance of wrinkles.

- **For oily or acne-prone skin**
  An oil-free long-lasting liquid will reduce shine and stay matte longer. To help fight acne, look for one that includes salicylic acid in the ingredients.

- **For sensitive and/or red skin**
  Opaque (meaning not able to see through) formulas can be found in liquid or stick form and provide the best coverage to hide any discolorations.

Setting Your Makeup

Since your skin dries out as you age, you may want to stop using powders because they can make you look drier and accentuate any fine lines. There are setting sprays available to keep your makeup looking great for hours without using a finishing powder. These sprays are a fine mist you spray over your made-up face. They seal in moisture and lock in your makeup. I got an organic formula on Amazon and my daughter loved it so much she also uses it now!

Eye Shadow and Liner

Eyelid primer will hold eye makeup in place so it does not get wiped off easily and prevents powdered eyeshadows from filling in and emphasizing wrinkles. Apply the primer all over the eyelid and under the eyes (I use mine very close to the edge of my lower eye to help hold my eyeliner in place too) prior to applying eyeshadow or foundation.

You can also shift away from the powder eyeshadow and use a crème eyeshadow on top of the primer for longer lasting, stay put eye makeup. To minimize emphasis on wrinkles around the eyes, reduce the frost or shimmer in your eyeshadow and shift into more of a mat finish or light sheen.

The same goes for eyeliners. Reduce the shiny and sparkly and go with a mid-tone liner with grey, brown, or soft colors. You can also use a soft touch of white eyeliner on the bottom rim and in the inner corners of your eyes which may help your eyes look a bit more open.

Special note: Make sure that you are also taking care to moisturize your eyelids. As we age, the eyelids thin and can get saggy and wrinkly so use a quality eye makeup remover and eye cream daily/nightly to help slow that process.

Lashes

We lose eyelash volume with age, so another key to look more youthful is to optimize your eyelashes. The best-known way and most obvious to most of us is to apply mascara.

Here are a few more tips that can help your lashes look great:

- Take care of the lashes you have by cleaning the mascara from your lashes each night. You can use an eye makeup remover solution or you can use liquid baby shampoo (this cleanses without irritating your eyes and was recommended to me by my ophthalmologist). Whichever you choose, apply to a cotton swab and gently wipe to remove the makeup. Be careful not to pull too much on this delicate eye skin or you can stretch the skin over time and actually cause more wrinkles.

- After your lashes are clean, make sure to condition them. One simple way to do this is to apply a high nutrient oil (castor oil is most commonly recommended) to your lashes with a cotton swab from root to tip each night.

- There are also premium lash enhancer serums to use on your lashes and/or brows each night which condition and develop the fullness, length, and color of your lashes.

- Latisse® is a prescription product that creates new lash growth. It is proven to work but does have risks associated with the discoloration of lighter colored eyes (the iris in the eye). You can talk with your dermatologist to get more information on if it is a good option for you.

False Eyelashes

You can apply false eyelashes to add more volume and length to your natural lashes. False eyelashes can be in the form of a full strip of lashes that attach as one piece across your eyelid, or individual false eyelashes inserted to specific spots within your own lashes. You can find "falsies" at your local drugstore, Amazon, or beauty shops.

There are also multiple lash spa locations opening up all around the country where you can have a professional apply lash extensions for you. If you want professional lash extensions simply run a search online for "Lash studio" or "Lash extensions" in your area. Be sure to read the reviews and make sure the environment is clean at the location you choose.

Teeth Whitening

Like your skin, your smile is one of the first things people will notice about you. There are simple ways to ensure your smile shines forth with confidence. Having your teeth as white and sparkly as possible will make you feel good every time you look in the mirror!

I know personally how this can make you feel more confident. When I was a child, my doctors put me on an antibiotic medication called Tetracycline. One of the major things they know about this drug now (but not when I was little) is that children younger than 8 years old should not take tetracycline because it can cause permanent tooth discoloration (and can also affect a child's growth). It creates grey stripy stains on the teeth.

My teeth were discolored for many years of my life. I tried several options at few different dentist offices and nothing seemed to help. After my divorce, I felt an even stronger desire to improve my teeth with the increased pressure I felt to look good as I started dating again.

After being told that nothing may work, and even considering cosmetic dentistry to get caps on my teeth, I tried Crest® 3D White™ Whitestrips™. I am not sure how or why, but they worked for me!

I now get complimented all the time on my smile and my teeth. My new dentist even commented on how white my teeth are! I continue to use them regularly to this day. They are much cheaper than the dentist solutions and easier, more convenient for me to do at home.

Although this is just my story and results will vary person to person, I included this in the book as an easy treatment that can be done by almost anyone anywhere for quick results and a big confidence boost.

That being said, there are many options available to whiten your teeth if you choose to do so. Options include: whitening toothpastes, trays, strips, and paint on solutions. Here is some additional info on options available:

A Dental Office

Every dental office today offers teeth whitening services. There are several types of whitening systems so ask about what each office offers. Some are done completely in office and some will give you a teeth mold to use at home with whitening solutions each day/week.

Whitening Strips

Crest®, Lumeeno™, and Harmony Life are some of the major brands but you can find other specialty brands too. I prefer the Crest® 3D White™ No Slip Whitestrips™ because they stick to my teeth better whereas some slide around and feel very uncomfortable and have less results. You can find many whitening strip varieties at your local store or on Amazon.com.

Pens and Paint-on Whitening Solutions

Go Smile®, Polar Teeth Whitening, AuraGlow, and Smilebriter, Colgate® Optic White® are some brands with whitening pens or brushes. With these, the whitening solution is applied tooth by tooth which avoids creating gum sensitivity as some other application types can. Although these products can be harder to find in stores, they are easily available for order on Amazon.com.

Whitening Kits/Systems

AuraGlow, Opalescence®, Go Smile®, Colgate® Optic White® are some of the major over the counter brands but there are many specialty brands available as well. Typically, a whitening kit or system will have multiple pieces and/or multiple steps. This includes things like kits with teeth trays to fill with gel and insert onto your teeth for a period of time, or kits with special lights, etc. You can find some of these through your dentist, or at some stores and at Amazon.com.

Natural Ways To Whiten Your Teeth

- **Baking Soda -** Just sprinkle a little baking soda in your hand or on a plate/bowl and dip your wet toothbrush in it to cover the bristles. Brush your teeth normally with this as desired. This helps to remove any build up on your teeth and keeps them feeling smooth and clean. I usually follow this up by brushing my teeth again with toothpaste to get that minty clean feeling. (For an all in one step, you can also mix the baking soda with your toothpaste.)

- **Activated charcoal** - Mix with water to form a paste and then apply the paste to your teeth and let sit for 2 minutes, then rinse by swishing with water until the charcoal is gone.

- **Oil pulling** - This is an old holistic remedy that helps to whiten your teeth and eliminate harmful bacteria in your mouth at the same time. You rinse your mouth with a spoonful of organic coconut oil (coconut oil has antibacterial properties).

  It will liquefy as it warms in your mouth; swish the oil back and forth in your mouth and gargle in the back of your throat like a mouthwash until it feels kind of thick and foamy. Then spit it out (into the trash can). You can repeat this as often as you like.

Special note: To avoid plumbing problems from buildup in your pipes, spit the oil out into the trashcan instead of your sink.

Grooming Your Private Area

Many cultures have different standards for how women maintain or groom their "private parts." It is a personal choice on how you "maintain your area," but if you are just getting back into the dating scene, this is a topic you may need to get updated on.

A study published in June of 2016 by JAMA Dermatology, found that 84% of all American women groomed their pubic hair and Cosmopolitan revealed in April 2017 that 57% of women age 18-35 went fully bare.

There are many ways to groom your lower region; here are some of the most popular styles and their descriptions.

Popular Hairstyle Options

- **The "Traditional" style** – removes the hair from the top and sides so nothing pokes out from your bikini bottom or panties.

- **The High Bikini or G-String** - removes more hair than the traditional on the sides and across the top and the back if requested.

- **The "Brazilian" or "The Hollywood"** - removes all hair down there (front, back, and between).

- **The Princess Cut** - leaves a vertical oval shape of hair (like a football).

- **The Landing Strip** – leaves a thin strip of hair running vertically down the center of the pubic region.

- **The Arrow** - leaves a landing strip with an arrowhead at the end pointing downward.

- **The Charlie Chaplin or Hitler** - leaves a straight strip of hair running horizontally across the top.

- **The Cardshark** - looks like a playing card with either hearts, diamonds, clubs, or spade shapes.

Trimming and Shaving:

If you plan to leave any hair in your private region, you will likely still want to at least trim up what is there. You can do this simply with a pair of scissors before you get into the bath or shower. Pull your hair away from your skin to cut it safely. Bathing after the trim will ensure you rinse off any loose hair clippings.

Shaving, if planned, can follow the trim while you are in the shower.

- Always use a sharp blade because a dull blade can cause bumps and ingrown hairs to form.

- Use shave gel or liquid bath wash to improve razor glide or use a razor with moisturizers built in.

- Do not work out immediately after you shave since sweat can sting your pores.

- Bump and Ingrown Hair Fighter solutions are available to help reduce skin conditions after a shave. You can find these at a drugstore next to hair removal kits or near the razors.

- Cortisone cream is a classic over the counter anti-itch medicine (cream, lotion, or ointment form). You can easily spread this on anywhere to minimize any itching you experience.

Bikini Wax

Waxing is the chosen method for many people because it is the least expensive way to remove hair that stays gone for as much as 4 weeks. Waxing can also be done on any part of the body where you want hair removed – I have friends that have waxed their eyebrows, legs, and arms too.

It can be painful the first few times but it gets easier the more times you do it. Generally, you will remain smooth and hair-free for about four weeks (depending. on the person). Even if you do not do it regularly, it is a great option prior to vacations or when schedules are extra busy so you can cut down your shower time.

When waxing is performed regularly, the natural hair growth will be reduced and the hair that grows back will be softer and finer reducing the formation of bumps or ingrown hairs.

Wax kits are available over-the-counter at many stores, however, I recommend going to a professional the first time you get a bikini wax. Ask friends for referrals or search "Bikini wax" near where you live on the internet. Read the reviews and ratings of the business before you book your appointment.

Typical Bikini Wax appointment:

The whole thing should only take about 30-60 minutes.

Special note: The waxer should wear gloves throughout your treatment. She should also use a different stick each time she dips into the wax so the wax stays clean and bacteria free from client to client.

- Wear comfy, soft panties to your appointment, because scratchy material may hurt or irritate your skin immediately after.

- You will asked to undress below the waist, lie down on a table, and bend one leg with your foot on the table and your knee up.

- The waxer will dip a clean stick into warm wax, apply it to a small section of your hair/skin, and then immediately press a strip of cloth onto the top of the warm wax. She will hold the cloth down for a few seconds while the wax cools and dries a bit, then, while holding the skin taut, she will pull the strip away with a quick tug. The wax and hair are removed with the strip.

- The waxer will immediately press on the treated area with her gloved hand to minimize any pain. The process continues many times until all desired areas have been done.

- After all has been stripped, the waxer will check for and remove any stray hairs with tweezers.

- Once done, the waxer will apply a soothing cream to your smooth skin.

- You will likely be red and tender in the treated areas for a few hours but that is normal.

- Apply a small amount of Cortisone cream, lotion, or ointment (from the drug store) to the skin if you experience any discomfort.

Bikini Laser Hair Removal:

Laser Hair Removal is more expensive than waxing but does provide excellent results that last much longer. A laser is used to kill the hair follicle which eliminates the hair from growing back. It is not totally permanent but can keep the area smooth and clean for months.

You will need multiple sessions to kill off all the follicles and keep the hair from coming back. Hair has three phases of growth cycle: Growth, Transition, and Resting. Since each individual hair can be in a different growth phase at any given time, not all hair follicles will react to the laser the same way at each appointment. It takes repeated sessions to damage all the hair follicles enough for them to stop producing hair.

The laser removal process may hurt a little bit (sort of a burning or stinging sensation). If you want to prevent any of these types of sensations, when you make the appointment tell the technician that you would like her to pre-apply the numbing cream before your treatment. She will likely ask you to arrive a bit early so they can apply that and give it a few moments to take effect before completing your treatment. They can also adjust the laser machine higher or lower for your tolerance level during the session.

After having your laser treatments once per month for about 4-6 months you will look and feel smooth and clean. Few hairs will be growing back and when they do they will be thinner and softer and less noticeable.

You will need to go in at least once per year for a touch-up to keep the hair from returning. But that is way better than shaving and waxing all the time and dealing with all the bumps, supplies, and time it takes to maintain daily otherwise. Like waxing, laser hair removal is not only for the bikini area. It can be used anywhere the body has dark hair.

Costs for laser hair removal can range based on your location and the size of the body area you have done. Many places will also offer discounts on the session price if you purchase a package of sessions up front. Another way to bring down the cost is to check on the daily coupon apps like Groupon.com or Livingsocial.com, etc. Laser hair removal is a common offering on these apps in many U.S. markets so check your location for options.

Before you make an appointment anywhere, spend time to check the reviews and the credentials of the business and make sure that a licensed practitioner will be performing the treatment with lasers specific for the job.

Here are a few things to know before you go to a laser hair removal session:

- **Do Not -** Tan the areas that will be treated because this can affect the treatment results and increase your chance of burn. (No self-tanning products either, nothing that darkens your skin.)

- **Do Not** - Pluck, wax, or bleach the area for at least 3 weeks prior to the treatment. Since the root and the hair pigment are critical for the laser to do its job, they must be there for the laser to work or that follicle will be missed during the treatment session.

- **Do Not** - Use any lotions or creams on the area the day of your appointment.

- **Do** – Shave the treatment area the morning of your appointment. This allows the laser to easily glide over the surface while sending the laser effects down along each hair and into the root to kill the follicle. The shaved areas also provide a visual template to the technician for where you want the hair removed.

- **Do** – The day of your appointment wash the area being treated completely and make sure there is no oil left on the skin.

- **Do** – Wear comfy, soft panties to your appointment to avoid any discomfort immediately afterwards.

Typical Laser Hair Removal appointment:

The whole thing should only take about 20-30 minutes.

Special note: The process works best on dark hair and will not work on blond or grey hair. For best results, go to a dermatologist or medical spa that uses lasers specifically designed for hair removal so you can get the best results.

- You will be asked to undress below the waist and lie down on a table.

- The therapist will provide sunglasses to wear as protection for your eyes from the laser light.

- The therapist will apply gel to the areas you want hair removed (they can tell which areas by where you have shaved but also speak up with your preferences). The gel helps the laser wand glide over your skin easily while keeping your skin cool during the procedure.

- The therapist will pass the laser wand over your skin, repeating the passes a few times for each section. Your skin will warm up and you will feel a prickly, stinging type of sensation.

- As she moves from spot to spot, she will apply more gel and re-position the wand to remove the unwanted hair.

- You may have a bit of redness for an hour or so immediately following the treatment but you will not get any bumps or ingrown hairs.

Cosmetic Surgery

This topic may be controversial and some women may have very valid reasons against cosmetic surgery. I discuss it here because for many women this is a valid and powerful option to gain back body confidence. If this choice is not for you please jump ahead to another section.

Cosmetic surgery does have its risks, but when done correctly you can be happy with your results for years to come. The confidence gained from modifying a feature that stirs feelings of insecurity in you can be a powerful life change and confidence booster. Facing the single world after coming out of a long relationship may leave you in a place where you feel self-conscious of your body. Sometimes, diet and exercise will not fix the areas we want to improve (like after childbirth) and cosmetic surgery may be the only option to create a change.

Cosmetic or what used to be called "plastic" surgery is growing in popularity. According to the 2017 American Society of Plastic Surgeons Report, 17.5 million cosmetic procedures were performed in the United States in 2017.

The Top 10 Plastic Surgery Treatments in 2017 as reported on www.harpersbazaar were:

1. Breast Augmentation / Lift
2. Rhinoplasty
3. Tummy Tuck
4. Liposuction
5. Vaginal Rejuvenation
6. Butt Enhancement
7. Facelift
8. Eyelid Surgery
9. Breast Reduction
10. Mommy Makeover (Breast & Tummy)

As you can see just from the list above there are many procedures available to "nip and tuck" just about every area of your body if you so choose. The lists here are far from comprehensive. If there is some part of your body you want to change do research online about the procedures available and the doctors who perform them.

Here are tips on how to handle your doctor selection process:

- Research the procedures available for your particular area of interest. Type in "Cosmetic procedures for XXX" (whatever body part you are searching for). You will have many listings show up. Read through the different options available to see what you are most comfortable with.

- During your research, you will likely come across different doctors that perform the procedure you have chosen. Make a list of the doctors you feel good about. Then search the doctors for ratings, articles, and reviews to ensure you feel comfortable with their experience. I know this all takes time but this is your body and it is worth the time to make sure you will be happy, healthy, and safe during and after the procedure.

- Make appointments with at least three doctors to meet them personally and get detailed custom written quotes for your specific requests. Make sure the quote includes the procedure and any anesthesia and/or surgery center costs so you will know your total out of pocket. Do not assume the highest price is the best but also beware of the doctor that is far less than the others.

Special note: If you are in a small town, think about heading into the city as this is a situation where you want to ensure the doctor has lots of experience with the procedure(s) for your area(s) of concern.

Ask the doctor EVERYTHING you want to know. This is not a place where you should feel stupid asking questions that pop into your mind. You must feel comfortable with the doctor and his answers to your questions.

I recommend taking a notepad and taking notes of each doctor's answers so it will make it easier to decide on which one (if any) you want to work with.

Here are some questions you may want to ask:

* Who will perform the procedure?
* How much will it cost?
* Is it all completed in one appointment or will you need to return for a series of appointments?
* Where is the location for the procedure to be done?
* What is the recovery time?
* What is the recovery process?
* What are the pre-procedure requirements (hygiene, diet, medicines, etc.)
* What are the post-procedure requirements?
* Are there any risks?

Cosmetic surgery can seem very scary so find a good doctor, follow all the instructions they give you for pre and post procedure and you will likely be very happy with the changes you have made. Everyone's needs are different so take the time to consider what is right for you before committing to any type of surgery.

Cosmetic Non-Surgical Procedures

I have put this section here because along with the cosmetic surgery section above, there are a number of procedures that can help you look your best at any age and that are non-invasive (meaning the procedure does not require an incision into the body). These procedures are generally performed in a doctor's office or at a medi-spa with an esthetician.

The Top Nine Non-surgical Treatments of 2017, again as reported on www.harpersbazaar.com, were:

1. Non-Surgical Fat Reduction (like Sculpsure™ and Coolsculpting®)
2. Fillers (like Juvederm® and Restylane®)
3. Hair Restoration
4. Toxins (Botox® and Dysport®)
5. Facial Lasers
6. Scar Treatment
7. Acne Treatment
8. Hair Removal
9. Chemical Peel

There are many treatments to enhance your beauty and/or battle the signs of aging. They vary widely by type, availability from office to office, and recovery times and costs.

New treatments continue to rapidly become available. Therefore, just like the surgical options, the best thing you can do if you are interested in finding a particular type of treatment or solution is to research the options online; read reviews, interview the doctors you select and get all the information you need to make the best decision for you.

Even with non-invasive procedures, there are many things you want to ask and evaluate before you make your decision(s):

- Who will perform the procedure?
- How much will it cost?
- Is it all completed in one appointment or will you need to return for a series of appointments?
- Where is the location for the procedure to be done?
- What is the recovery time?
- What is the recovery process?
- How long will the results last?
- Can you go right back to work or out straight after the appointment?
- What are the pre-procedure requirements (skin products, diet, medicines, etc.)
- What are the post-procedure requirements?
- Are there any risks?

Be Thoughtful.

_____

_____

_____

_____

_____

_____

_____

_____

_____

_____

_____

Be Thoughtful.

_____

_____

_____

_____

_____

_____

_____

_____

_____

_____

_____

Be Thoughtful.

_____

_____

_____

_____

_____

_____

_____

_____

_____

_____

———————

Be Safe.

"A prudent man foresees the difficulties ahead and prepares for them; the simpleton goes blindly on and suffers the consequences." ~Proverbs 22:3	"Any intelligent fool can make things bigger, more complex, and more violent. It takes a touch of genius — and a lot of courage - to move in the opposite direction." ~ Albert Einstein	Hindsight is a wonderful thing but foresight is better, especially when it comes to saving life, or some pain! ~ William Blake
Safety doesn't happen by accident. ~Author Unknown	Precaution is better than cure. ~Edward Coke	Prepare and prevent, don't repair and repent. ~Author Unknown
Your safety gears are between your ears. ~Author Unknown	Don't learn safety by accident. ~Author Unknown	It is better to be safe than sorry. ~American Proverb
"Out of clutter find simplicity; from discord find harmony; In the middle of difficulty lies opportunity" ~ Einstein	"You cannot change what you refuse to confront" ~Unknown	"By failing to prepare, you are preparing to fail." ~Benjamin Franklin

SAFETY

Ok, safety may not be your favorite topic. I know it isn't mine. I would much rather discuss happy or inspirational topics and ignore anything that I find disturbing. However, this is a critical area for you, and all women, to have information that empowers your decisions and actions.

There is a broad array of topics covered in this section. Some may be new to you, some may be refreshers, and some of the information may be disturbing to read but I would be leaving a big gaping hole in your guidebook if I did not address these safety topics.

Data

Let's start with the topic of data. With over 25 years in database marketing, I know where and how data is collected and how it is used. Since we live in an information society, data collection is everywhere. You likely know that there are companies out there that collect data on every single person living in the United States and many parts of the world. You, and information about you, is in multiple databases in multiple systems, in multiple places, worldwide.

Companies can know where you live, who you live with, if you have children, how old they are, where you work, what you buy, how frequently you buy it, what you read, what you listen to, what you eat, where you eat it, what credit card you use and what you buy with it, what your balances are in your accounts, how you pay your bills, what organizations you are a member of, what political views you have, if you own a pet, what kind of car you use, what brands you like to buy, what apps you use, what device you engage on, if you use coupons, if you eat junk food, your hobbies, where you go each day, and so on.

I intentionally made the list above long to share only a small portion of the many details about you available to anyone. What you may not know is that two of the best ways to identify you and match you to all of these details (and more) is with your cell phone number and/or your email address.

That is important for you to know so you are empowered to think more fully about giving your personal phone number out or personal email address out to strangers. I am not saying you should not share your contact information with people you want to be in contact with and get to know. I am saying, before you do, just pause and think about it and your comfort level with the person or company you are giving it to. Strong consideration should be given to giving out your personal information to people from online dating sites, or at a bar. I highly recommend taking time to message them through an app or website before you give them your information.

One way to handle this is to create a separate FB page, or other social media account, and/or email account where you post general or professional information, but keep your personal life separate. When you want to create a connection with someone new, use this account. This will allow you to message with people through a safe platform as you get to know them. Since they will have to accept your friend request, it also will allow you to see into more of their world and profile so you can become comfortable with giving them your phone number or email at a later time.

Special Note: Read more on this in the section on social media later in this book.

Apps

Any app you have on your phone, tablet, or computer is collecting data on you. This is especially true of "free" apps. Nothing is really free; they are getting something back and that valuable asset is all the data they collect about you. Be selective about what you download to your phone, tablet, or computer.

Also, when installing something and the box comes up that says "this app wants to have access to…location, contacts, camera, photos, etc." Take a moment to read it. If the app is important to you, then you may need to accept the terms. If not, you can rethink the download, and look for a different app that does what you are looking for without all the permission access requested.

Sometimes the app allows you to choose what information or functions you give the app access to. Unless necessary for the app to run, consider denying it access to your location and your contacts. Location sharing is a common feature of many apps and cell phone operating systems and it can be helpful and/or fun but you may not want everyone to know where you are all the time (especially if you have shared your phone number with people you are just getting to know). Also remember that any app that has access to your location will store the information about where you have been, every minute of every day while your location sharing is enabled.

Passwords

Do not save your passwords on apps and websites, especially for financial accounts! You know, when the little pop up shows asking if you want it to remember your password – always say no. I know this may seem like an inconvenience but it is nothing compared to someone hacking into your accounts and/or stealing your identity. Keep your passwords safe and private. Hackers can get into even the world's biggest financial institution databases so you do not want your passwords stored anywhere out there just for convenience.

Social Media

Social media becomes more a part of our lives every year. If you have children, they do not even remember life without it! Social media is fun and does such a great job of connecting us all and allows us to share information efficiently with large groups of people. I have had so much fun reconnecting with friends from my past and have learned quite a bit from people, groups or pages I have followed.

As a single woman, if you have social media accounts where you post personal things about you and your family, be very specific with who you friend or accept to follow you. According to the Centers for Disease Control, 1 in 6 women will be cyberstalked in her lifetime so this is important safety information for all women.

- Never accept a friend request from someone you don't know, even if the app shows them as having mutual friends with you. You do not want to give strangers access to your personal posts. (Identity thieves can even create fake profiles to get information on you).

- Be careful about filling out posts and quizzes that reveal personal information about you. Many of these quizzes ask things like: What was your first pet's name? Do you remember your childhood phone number? What street did you grow up on? These are the same type of questions that are used as security questions for many accounts. Be cautious. Even if they seem like fun, quizzes that collect this type of information can give people a lot of personal information about you that will be stored online forever.

- If you want to use social media for work or even to keep connected with new people you meet (or date), set up more than one social networking account: one for your personal life and one for your more public persona. Make sure your family/friends know to post only to your personal account, not your public one.

- Do not allow apps access to all of your contacts or your email address book.

There is no such thing as "private" anymore. Since anything posted on the internet may be there forever, consider controlling more of what you allow to be posted on your accounts. Make sure your privacy settings are set to enable you to review any content in which you've been tagged before it is posted on your page. Facebook and many other social media sites allow people to tag others on posts at places and times even if they are not there together. Do not hesitate to delete something that from your account because you are fearful of hurting someone's feelings. Tell the person privately why you took it down, but remember you must do what you feel is right for you, with courage and kindness, not just for your online persona today but also considering how it will be perceived over time.

Identity Protection

Your identity is more than your personal being or reputation. Your identity joins who you are with what you have built, what you own, and who you are connected to. More specifically it can include your financial records, medical history, education records, travel records, social media profiles, citizenship, professional, contact, government, and legal records. Because we live in a digital world, there are few in-person transactions so if someone gets enough of your personal information, they can pretend to be you in cyberspace. We cannot hide or pretend these threats do not exist (as much as you and I may want to!)

In September 2017, Equifax one of the big three United States Credit Bureaus had a data breach that affected approximately 143 million Americans (almost every adult in the US). Once hacked, the only thing a company can do is notify you and other financial institutions that your personal identity may be in question.

Hackers know that financial companies are great targets since not only is this where the money is, but also our lifelong personal identifiers (like SS# in the U.S.). Since this same identifier is used to identify you at multiple entities throughout the world, it will connect your information from multiple different databases into one profile of your life. These identifiers can give criminals access to your identity and most aspects of your life.

Whatever your situation or phase of life, protecting your identity and your financial assets is critical to living a life you love. Here is the simplest summary of what you must know to protect your identity and/or react to any breach that occurs.

- **Check your own credit report at least once per year and fix any errors** - all Americans can get a free copy of their credit reports once a year through <u>AnnualCreditReport.com.</u>

- **Look through your postal mail** - Make sure no surprises show up in account statements or letters.

- **Change your passwords regularly** - at least once per year and anytime you feel that there may have been a breach.

- **Verify your financial account information regularly** - check the accuracy of your address and other profile points and the activity on the account: purchases, withdrawals, money wires, credit-line increases, escalating balances, etc.

- **Set-up email alerts** - many accounts will offer a notification service to alert you whenever purchases exceed a certain dollar amount. This can be helpful if you are notified of a purchase you did not make. You may also limit the dollar amount that can be wired from your bank accounts without your being physically present.

- **Create strong passwords** - although annoying to have to include capitals and symbols and numbers in your password, it helps prevent hackers from getting into your accounts. Also, whenever possible, set up personal identification numbers (PIN) and use multi-factor authentication options to strengthen the security on your accounts.

- **Do not stay logged in or save passwords on any online browsers or search engines** - That defeats the purpose of the password as being needed each time someone tries to access the account. And never give your passwords or PINs to anyone.

- **Back up your phone** - Since your cell phone contains so much data about you, if you lose it your personal information could be threatened. Apple iPhones and Google Android phones have features that allow you to remotely lock or wipe your phone contents clean ("Find My iPhone" and "Android Lost") in case of an emergency. To avoid emotional stress over the loss of everything, make sure to keep your phone backed up regularly.

Identity theft protection services

There are several different professional monitoring and protection services available. A comprehensive identity theft protection service should include ways to help prevent fraud, clean up any issues that arise from fraud, and inform you if your personal information has been used to commit fraud.

Comprehensive identity protection services monitor things like:

Bank accounts	Credit reports
Credit/debit cards	Social Security number
Medical Information	Passport
Email Accounts	The Dark Web

Three of the most highly ranked identity theft protection companies to check out in America are:

- IdentityForce
- ID Watchdog
- LifeLock

Fraud Alerts

Fraud alerts are subscription-based services that alert you to "suspicious" activity on your financial accounts. The service will watch for things like when your credit is checked for large purchases, when a new account is opened in your name, or when new loans are processed.

Your fraud protection company will also notify potential creditors to use additional security steps to verify your identity before processing any requests that will affect your credit. Most services also include access to copies of your credit reports from all 3 U.S. credit bureaus.

A few basic fraud alert services you can get for free:

- Experian offers a 30-day Identity Theft Protection Alert service for free.

- "Experian IdentityWorks[SM]" service includes things like credit monitoring, Dark Web surveillance, credit locks, identity theft insurance, fraud resolution support, FICO® score trackers, etc. The first 30 days are free but then it will automatically turn into a monthly subscription if you do not cancel it.

- Equifax offers a free 90-day fraud alert service. You can set a new one up every 90 days for free or you can purchase their fraud alert subscription.

Special note: There are many ways to get covered for identity theft. Besides subscribing to a service separately, check to see if you are covered by your credit union or with membership in organizations such as AAA.

You may also be covered under your homeowner's or renter's insurance policy or you may be able to add coverage to your policy. Some companies even offer identity-theft protection or credit monitoring as part of employee benefits packages so check your HR benefits with your employer.

Credit Freeze

This is not a notification service. A credit freeze actually locks your credit history and only allows your current creditors to view it for already existing accounts. That means that if you put a freeze in place no one new will be able to view your credit report. This is an effective way to prevent unknown financial actions in your name, but if you want an employer, landlord, or school to review your credit you will first have to "thaw" out your credit by making a formal request to the company you have the freeze with and pay them any required fees.

If You Suspect Identity Theft

If you suspect you have been a victim of identity theft fraud and you have no comprehensive protection service, you must report it to the credit bureaus AND take the following steps to notify the other parties:

- ## The 3 Major Credit Unions

  Quickly file a report with one of the credit bureaus. The law requires that they will each share this information with the other two. A "Fraud Alert" will be automatically placed on your file and no new credit will be granted without your approval.

  TransUnion: 1-800-680-7289

  Equifax: 1-800-525-6285

  Experian: 1-888-397-3742

• Credit Card Companies

When you report fraud or the loss of your card to the credit card company it limits your financial risk. Timing is important. If you report it before anyone uses the card you will be cleared of any liability to pay back the funds due to unauthorized use. Otherwise, you may have to pay part or all of the monies back depending on your credit card policy.

Mastercard: 800-MC-ASSIST

Visa: 800-847-2911

• ATM/ Debit Card

Lost (or stolen) ATM and Debit cards must be reported immediately to protect your money. Your liability for withdrawals and charges to the card increase the longer the card is lost. It also gives thieves more time to commit fraud by using the card.

Here is a typical timeline on coverage and liabilities for losses incurred:

o   Report your lost/stolen card before someone uses it and you are not held liable for any unauthorized withdrawals.

o   Report your lost/stolen card within 2 business days and your financial loss/liability is limited.

- Report your lost/stolen card after 2 business days, but within 60 days and your financial loss/liability is limited but you will have less money returned to your account.

- After 60 days any money that was charged/taken out of your account will likely not be protected or returned to you = Total Loss.

• Federal Trade Commission (FTC)

Submit a report to the FTC at
www.ftc.gov or 1-877-ID-THEFT

• Social Security Administration (SSA)

Report any suspicious activity to the SSA immediately.

Fax: 410-597-0118

Phone: 1-800-269-0271

U.S. Mail: Social Security Fraud Hotline
P.O. Box 17785
Baltimore, Maryland 21235

Internet: Fraud Reporting Form
https://www.ssa.gov/fraudreport/oig/pub
lic_fraud_reporting/form.htm

- **United States Postal Service**

  Notify the postal system so they are aware of any suspected fraud and can stop any incorrect change of address activity before the change gets processed.

  Phone: 1-800-ASK-USPS®
  1-800-275-8777

- **Police Report**

  Identity theft is a federal crime and should be reported to the police department. Contact your local police department to complete a police report. This will also be important to you as an official record of the occurrence(s) to help you recover any losses or costs incurred in the recovery process.

Dating

Let's face it; the dating process today differs from 20, 15, 10, or even 5 years ago! To set you off on the right track you must be aware of many of the typical mainstream tools, assumptions, and pitfalls of this modern dating environment to stay empowered and live happy, healthy, and safe.

When you are ready, dating can be a huge growth experience. Meeting new people, hearing new perspectives, seeing new ways of living, going to new places, and experiencing new things can open up your view of the world. It can be very exciting and a bit overwhelming at times as well.

As we talked about in other sections of this book, taking time to define what you want and the vision you have for your life and your relationships is key in making those visions come true for you. The clearer you are about what you want the more you can align your actions and decisions to achieve all that you desire.

Take time to consider what you want in your romantic partner.

You know when you shop for a home, they recommend you make a list of your "Must haves" and then your "Wish to haves"? This is similar. You must know what the "deal-breakers" are for you. The things you absolutely will not accept in a partner, and those few things you absolutely must have. This prepares you to make empowered choices about who you choose to date which will reduce stress and disruption in your dating life and increase your enjoyment. Since the items on your list should be based on your deep-rooted needs and values, use these as your guiding principles for dating.

Activity: Create a short list of your "must haves" and "must not haves" in your ideal partner. This list should be short and contain no more than 3-5 qualities that your ideal match must have and 3-5 qualities they must not have. You may think of many things initially for these categories, so write them all down. Then you must prioritize your list under each category (Must or Must Not) and eliminate down to the top "deal-breakers." Use your list as a mental checklist when considering going on a date with someone new.

Do not date people that do not meet these basic requirements. There is no benefit in getting involved with someone you know does not meet your basic needs. That will only create unneeded drama in your life.

To get more specific, here is one possible example:

Must Have/Be	**Must Not Have/Not Be**
Have positive attitude	Not smoke/do drugs
Be trustworthy/open	Not Selfish/Narcissistic
Have grown children	Not have cheated before
Active lifestyle /Enjoy travel	Not have anger issues

Don't fall into the disempowering trap that many women find themselves in when they meet new people; do not focus on *if the other person likes you*. The empowered position is to flip that thinking around to instead focus on *figuring out if you like them*! Let me say that again because for many women this is a huge mindset shift – don't focus on figuring out if they like you, focus on figuring out if you like them! Acknowledge that you are powerful in the choices you make and that it is important to choose the people you want to spend time with.

First and foremost, spend time discovering if they meet the requirements on your "Must have" and "Must not have" lists. Do you feel energized when you are with them? Are they interested in what you have to say? Are you interested in what they have to say? Do you enjoy their company? Are you attracted to them? Do you respect them? If these are all yes answers, then over time guide the conversations and activities with them to explore if you enjoy similar activities, social patterns, family involvement, religious views, charitable views, travel styles, and saving/spending patterns. These are all valuable questions for you to consider. Remember you have a choice in every aspect of your life. You actively choose who you love. Decide what you want and who you want, then keep choosing the actions, environments, and people that will be a part of your vision. Deciding and taking the actions aligned with the vision of what you want, is how you will get there.

When dating new people, there may be times that you determine early in the encounter the person will not be someone you want to see again. Be powerful to take the actions you must to stay happy, healthy, and safe and act with courage and kindness. Stay aligned with your vision. Do not give them mixed signals or allow yourself to become confused by getting affectionate with them.

If your goal is to build a loving relationship with someone, do not get sexual with them until you have had time to determine if this person (1) meets your basic requirements, (2) is someone you have deemed with high potential for being your ideal partner and who is worthy of your time. Sexual activity triggers biological reactions in your body. For women, those reactions can make it much harder to remove ourselves from situations we later find we don't want to be in. It is different for men they do not have those same biological effects from sex. You will create drama and stress for yourself if you become sexual before you have gotten to know if the person you are with is someone you want to be with. Although it can be difficult to be patient, if there is strong potential for a deeper relationship with this person, then taking time to learn who they are and the growing anticipation of being with them can be fun.

Special note: Always remember that if you have children, they must be your priority. Make sure they feel comfortable around new people you introduce to them – whether that is new friends or new love interests. These are your children and they will be molded by everything they experience with you. Our children look to us as their mother for love and stability. So, do what is right for you, but with courage and compassion for others in your life. Take it as slow as possible to introduce your children to new men. Take care to be selective about who they meet and ensure as much as possible that their first meeting with someone new is in a situation that will be a foundation for a pleasant relation between all of you (not, for example, an unannounced/unplanned guest at the front door, or at the breakfast table one morning).

Online Dating

Online dating began in 1995 when Match.com was founded as the first official online dating site. Since then many dating sites have been created and millions of people have participated in online dating platforms to find love and/or sex. Online dating has become main stream. It is now an accepted and common way for people to meet other people.

Although it provides many benefits in creating opportunities to meet new people, like anything, it also has some pitfalls. Statistics show that over 50% of all online daters are already/currently in a relationship of some kind and that sex offenders also use online dating to meet people.

Online dating is the opposite of what we were taught as kids when our parents said, "Never talk to strangers." When communicating through online dating sites you do not know who you are communicating with. You don't know if their profile is the truth or a bunch of lies. You don't know their history, or their friends, or even their name. Remember all of this because as you message and text people and look at their photos, you can develop a "false sense of familiarity" with the person so that when you meet them, you feel like you know them, but you don't.

If you give online dating a go, there are steps you should take to keep yourself safe and have the best experiences possible.

- Set up a separate email address for use only with online dating site accounts.

- Be honest and positive on your profile and use your best, recent photos. Don't set yourself up for disappointment or humiliation by presenting yourself as something online that will not be true in person.

- Use the messaging interface within your online dating platform to communicate with the people you are interested in prior to giving them your personal email or phone numbers.

- Have a "system" for filtering the people you want to (and do not want to) engage with.

Online-dating Filtering System

Here is an example of a filtering system to set up for your process of evaluating potential dates through online platforms. This is just a sample, create one that works for you and your needs.

- Once you connect with someone online, message within the system back and forth for a few days or even a week(s). The system keeps your personal information private and gives you time to determine if you want to share your contact information. Be cautiously optimistic.

- Never give your phone number first – always get theirs first so you can enter it into your phone so you know who is calling you. Wait for them to ask for your number, but when they do, tell them you need theirs first. (When you save their contact info into your phone make sure you include their real name, their online profile name, and what site you met them on as this may be helpful information later.)

- After you have exchanged phone numbers, talk on the phone together for at least 20-30 minutes. This is a conversation about getting to know each other, NOT just about setting logistics to meet.

- Google them. This only takes a moment and can help give you a feel for who they are professionally, and validate some of the information they have shared with you already.

- If you feel like you connect and that the other person seems trustworthy then set the meetup time and place. Make sure this is a public place where you feel safe.

- Do not have them come to your place to pick you up for your first meeting. (You may not want them to know where you live after you meet them).

- When you go to meet someone from an online dating service for the first time make sure at least one adult in your life knows where you are going and who you will be meeting.

Special note: There are many people online that will try to rush the process you have designed for your filtering system. If these people do not want to honor these steps with you, move on and select someone else. An impatient or pushy person online will be impatient and pushy in-person also.

Looking for a Potential Date

The things to look for in someone's online profile descriptions are the same things you would look for in someone when you meet them live and in person. Here are some suggestions:

- **Basics** - Do they meet your basic requirements? Get the answers to these qualities before you ever meet with them. You need not go on a date with someone you already know does not meet your basic guidelines.

- **Positivity** - Do they seem happy and approach life with optimism or are they ranting about past relationships, the government, their job, etc.?

- **Religion/Spirituality** - Do they include their religious beliefs in their profile? Do they match your religious beliefs? Do they express this openly? Do you like that?

- **Openness/Honesty** - Do they seem open and honest in their written profile and in your messaging back and forth? Does the profile seem to synch up with the person in photos?

- **Similar Interests** - Do they talk about hobbies and interests you like, or have an interest in trying?

- **Kids/No kids** - You may not be able to tell if they want kids from their profile but if they have them, are you ok with that situation?

- **Lifestyle cues** - From what you can tell, through photos and your communication, does it seem like you have/want similar lifestyles? Do they have a pet? What job do they have? Do they share your religious beliefs? Does their education level fit what you want?

- **A sense of attraction** - Do you have a sense of attraction to them? Do they appeal to you in their worst photo and their best photo?

- **Photos** - Many things may not be written in words. Don't just look at the person in the photos, look at the environment around them too. Where are they? Who are they with? Are they alone in all of them? Is he with friends?

Special note: Pictures can sometimes create a story in your head since our brains will fill in gaps of unknown information. Do not assume what you interpret from the photos is the full reality. It may/may not be their dog, their house, their boat, their car. For example: you may innocently assume the photo is taken at their home when in reality it may have been at a friend or family member's house, from a recent vacation, etc. Just use the photo cues to ask questions and create conversation to learn more about them and their lifestyle.

Your Online Dating Profile

So now you know what to look for initially in the bio to find prospective dates that appeal to you. What should you put in yours to attract them to you? There are many ways to create a profile that appeals to others.

Here are some guidelines for the content of your bio and how to present your story.

- **Honesty -** First and foremost be honest. Yes, you should put your best foot forward, but don't say things that are not true or imply things that are inaccurate.

  For example, if you want to list an activity you have only done once then say something like "I recently XXX and can't wait to do it again..." or I tried XXX and would like to do it more." Don't say "I do yoga" if you only have done it once or the last time you did it was 10 years ago.

- **Positivity** - Remember we talked about this being something for you to look for as you search through prospective profiles? Well, the same goes for you. Keep your tone as upbeat and happy as you can. Re-read your words and shift anything that takes a negative tone to sound more positive. For example, instead of saying you haven't traveled much; say there are many places you want to go.

- **Relationships** - Do NOT mention previous relationships in your profile. It is not appropriate to include all those personal details in a computer profile that many strangers will be viewing. Instead describe your vision of the relationship you are looking for and the qualities you want in your future partner.

- **Interests and Hobbies** - Since many people will skim through your profile and not read all of it, include the things you are most passionate about up front. If you enjoy many different activities, try using a bulleted list format so it stands out and they can read it quickly. A few items that have been reported to attract others to a profile are: outdoors and sporty activities, cooking, being a "foodie," and travel.

- **Stories** - Stories about you in embarrassing, fun, or proud situations is a fun way to share information with readers and helps them visualize what life would be like with you.

- **Goals/Dreams** - Sharing things you are trying to accomplish in the next year or so helps them visualize things they may be a part of in the future. It can also help generate some interesting conversations and create the opportunity for you to inquire about their goals and future plans.

- **Age** - I know many women want to "round down" on their age but you do not want to start a relationship with a lie. What if it takes off and you get serious and they see your driver's license or passport? Don't' undermine their trust before you even meet. I understand that because of the search algorithms in the online dating site you may want to show up in more searches by putting a younger age.

I suggest the following solution:
In the main profile settings that drive the search, put whatever age you want. But then in your profile description – at the top – include a note that the age entered was not right and you want anyone reading your profile to know that you were born in XXXX year.

If they are interested and continue to read through your profile they can decide whether to contact you with all the facts available. This will allow you to enjoy the process and not be stressed because you feel like you are hiding anything from the people you communicate with.

- **Children -** If you have children mention them but do NOT post pictures that include your children. This is not the place to expose your minor child(ren) to a bunch of strangers from all over the world, country, county, city, or town.

- **Keep your profile concise -** Use no more than four short paragraphs and/or bulleted lists in your profile to share your interests and what you are looking for in a relationship.

- **Editing -** Always ensure that the grammar and punctuation are correct in your profile. Many people get irritated by typos and errors. Since you want to make a good first impression to as many readers as possible, take the time to check and edit your writing. If the platform does not have spell check capabilities, you can copy and paste your written bio into Word or use the Grammarly app/website to check for spelling and grammar errors so you can fix them before you post your bio content.

- **Update your profile regularly -** You want your profile to accurately show who you are so as things change your profile should reflect that. Profiles that get updated are also served up more often to viewers by the dating platforms so by changing things up your profile will have more chances of being seen and you will have more opportunities to be contacted.

- **Sex** - Whether to include sexual innuendos in your profile or initial messages with someone online depends really on what you are hoping to get out of the online experience.

  Remember these people do not know you. They do not know if you are making a light-hearted joke or if you are serious about your sexual references. If you are looking for a hookup you may feel comfortable including more sexual references. If you are looking for a longer lasting relationship it is better to eliminate these comments from your profile and wait until you get to know them before you imply anything.

Writing Your Dating Profile

Sometimes it can be difficult to write your personal bio so here are a few strategies to get your thoughts and profile writing flowing:

- **Lists** - Include a list of things that excite you.
  - Places you want to go.
  - Things you want to see or do.
  - Your favorite music bands/songs, books, movies, foods, or sports teams you love.

- **Ask your friends** - Reach out to people you trust and ask them how they would describe you to someone? Listen to what they say and include some of their descriptions in your bio.

- **Video -** Pick an event that happened in your life and video tape yourself telling the story. (Sometimes it is easier to tell a story out loud.) Then you can go back to it and listen for details to include in your profile.

Special note: You can also use this same method to describe something that you dream of happening in your future. The key is to make sure it is listed as a dream or goal in your bio, then include lots of details to help the reader visualize it all in their mind. Include things like: what you are doing, where you are, when will it happen, how you will feel, what you will see, taste, hear, smell?

Your Dating Profile Photos

The most important thing when you choose your profile photos is to make sure they are a true representation of what you look like now.

I can't think of a more awkward and embarrassing experience than to meet up with someone and have them be upset and/or not recognize you because you posted an inaccurate photo of yourself and they were expecting to see a different you.

Here are a few tips to help your photos stand out, in a positive way:

- **Post recent photos -** Photos within the last year are best. If you don't have any you like, go take one. You need at least one good recent photo for your main profile picture. You can post a few that are older, but label them with at least the year they were taken so you are not implying they are current.

- **Face the camera** - Include photos where you are looking into the camera. People want to see your face. Do not include more than one photo of you wearing sunglasses. It is important for them to see your eyes because it can help create a sense of connection with you.

- **Show your smile** - Just like your eyes, your smile will draw viewers in. People love to see photos of happy people smiling and laughing. Surveys show that a smile where you show your teeth attracts significantly more people than a closed mouth smile or sexy pout. Photos of you laughing can help the viewer imagine having a great time being with you.

- **Let it be you** - Your main profile picture should be of you only. Never use a bathroom photo or selfie for this picture though. Ask friends or family to take a few pictures of you, or you can always go out in public somewhere, stop someone, and ask them to take a few photos of you. Tourists do it all the time!

- **Be social** - Include photos of you having fun in a group also. These can be fun shots with friends, coworkers, or family.

- **Show yourself in action** - Include some photos of you doing what you love. Showing yourself involved in activities that you describe in your bio helps to verify in their mind the lifestyle you enjoy and allows them to visualize being with you doing those things. Studies show that photos of women in sports/outdoor activities generate the highest response from men, however, if you love to curl up with a good book or paint, or garden, show photos of you doing those things. The point is to show who you are in order to find people who appreciate you for you.

- **Be complete** - Add at least one photo that shows your full body. Since this leaves no question in their mind on what you look like, they can be comfortable communicating with you and it will be much more enjoyable for you to talk with people when you know you have nothing to hide. You will feel confident accepting the dates and meeting the people you choose to meet.

- **Post multiple photos** - More photos give people more visibility into your life so they can see you in different looks, angles, places, and situations. It also provides ques for conversations while you get to know each other. Since many people don't read the whole profile, or forget the words, photos are a great way to get noticed, and be remembered. Shoot for five to nine good photos.

Special note: Remember you need to ensure your safety above all. Ultimately you are posting personal things for strangers to see. Do not post pictures with children and also crop out or cover up personal or contact information like names, phone numbers, school/team names, or addresses.

List of Dating Sites

Here are a few of the biggest general dating sites:

- eHarmony.com
- Match.com
- Okcupid.com
- POF.com (Plenty of Fish)

There are also more niche sites available if you are looking for a certain partner. Here are just a few (this list is no way complete and new sites can be created all the time so search online with your specific keywords):

- **African American Sites:**
    - BlackSingles.com:
    - BlackPeopleMeet.com
    - Afrointroductions.com

- **Christian Sites:**
    - ChristianMingle.com
    - ChristianCafe.com
    - ChristianCupid.com

- **Gay and Lesbian Dating Sites:**
    - GayCupid.com

- o   PinkCupid.com

- **Interracial Dating Sites:**
  - o   InterracialMatch.com
  - o   InterracialCupid.com

- **Jewish Dating Sites:**
  - o   Jdate.com

- **Latin Dating Sites:**
  - o   LatinAmericanCupid.com
  - o   Amigos.com

- **Senior Dating Sites**
  - o   SeniorPeopleMeet.com

- **Single Parent Dating Sites**
  - o   SingleParentMeet.com

Tips Specific to Tinder

Tinder differs from the online dating sites described above because it is a location-based mobile dating app driven mainly by photos. The system works by showing you photos of prospective dates and their age, distance, and a short bio.

If you are interested in the person shown, you swipe the photo right and if you are not, you swipe the photo left. When both people swipe right on each other the system sends both people a message that says "You are a Match!" Because the photos are the most important piece of this process, the way you set up your profile differs from the online dating websites.

Since Tinder is a photo-based app, your photos may be the only thing that people see on Tinder to decide if they are interested in you. Post at least three good pictures but, similar to online dating platforms, if you post more photos you will increase your chances of getting matches.

- Put your best picture first. Make sure it is clear and shows your face smiling and looking happy (Never use a selfie or a bathroom mirror photo). The other photos you choose can be group shots and/or photos showing you doing activities you love.

- The Tinder bio has a short 500-character limit. Write a brief statement about you, something you are passionate about, or what you are looking for. Do not leave this blank.

- When Tinder notifies you of a match, remember that it means there is a mutual interest. This is where the one-to-one communication can begin.

   Be honest about what you are looking for, but remember not to give out your phone number or address information right away. Try chatting within the app for a while so you can decide if you want to get to know them more personally and/or meet up with them somewhere.

Going Out Single

As a newly single woman, you will be headed out for many new experiences on your own, with your girlfriends, with dates, and around many new people. This can be exhilarating and fun. To enjoy yourself, stay empowered, and live happy, healthy, and safe, there are a few things to consider when you go out, especially if you are out with people you do not know well.

- Never leave a public place with someone you do not know or have just met.

- When you are with new people, don't leave your food or drink alone; either finish it or take it with you...even if you must take a glass to the bathroom. If you come back to the table and your drink is now full don't drink it. A simple way to handle this is to ask for something different, or say there is a hair or something in the glass, and get a new drink. This includes your water glass.

- If someone offers to buy you a drink, listen and watch the order and the delivery of your drink to ensure it is fresh and untainted.

- If a drink gets delivered to you by a stranger, do not drink it. You can say you would prefer something else and get a new drink, or just don't drink it.

- If you feel like you are being pressured to drink, leave your drink and get away from the situation. Go join another group, or leave the venue altogether.

Special Note: Pressure to drink can be verbal with someone telling or asking you to drink more, or it can be subtle with someone quickly and consistently refilling your drink or buying you new rounds.

- Water bottles are great at big events with lots of people you do not know. Buy bottled water or take your own water bottle and keep the cap on it. If you want to refill it, do it yourself from the tap. Tap water may seem gross but it can be safer than having it refilled from/by a source you are unsure of.

- Always make sure that your car has enough gas and/or electric charge before you go out. You don't want to get stranded and it can be uncomfortable and dangerous to stop at a gas station to fill up late at night (especially when dressed in your night out clothing).

- Take a wrap, sweater or jacket in case you get cold and in case you ever feel uncomfortable and want to cover up. I always take a wrap or scarf and will frequently tie it to the strap on my purse so I do not have to keep track of it if I don't need it.

Background Information

Landlords, employers, and financial institutions all run background checks on strangers. Dating people you know very little about can raise many questions in your mind, so don't feel bad about researching someone new you are just getting to know. There are many different types of sources you can review if you want to learn more about a person you have met online, at a bar, or anywhere else.

Information can help guide you but always remember that you know what is best for you. If your gut says there is something wrong, or you see bad patterns that the person engages in, remove yourself from that situation and do not go back. Your safety (physical and mental wellbeing) is critically important to your happiness.

Search Engines

Google may be the first place you think to search for information on someone, but there are other search engines like Bing or Yahoo also that have different content and different search algorithms which means you will likely get different results for the same search. Go to the search engine and enter the person's name + city + age, etc. Search on a few different combinations of information you have about them. If you see posts from their social site profiles come up, go to the site and look for their account. Even if their account is private there may be portions that are public (for example Facebook makes all profile photos public.)

Google Image Search

You can also run a Google search based on images. Open the Google Images home page and drag an image from your computer or a social media site over to the Google page.

A window will pop up and you drop the image into the box which will immediately kick off a search for similar images. Although this is super easy to run, there is a possibility that you get no relevant image results. When I searched for my image all that came up was the definition of "blonde" and images of other blonds – nothing with me.

Social Accounts

Social accounts are a fun way to get to know someone because you may see photos of their activities, career/business, friends, and additional profile information.

Look for posts that describe/show their likes, dislikes and attitudes to see if you like their viewpoints and if things seem to match up to what you have learned about them. When you look at them in the photos consider the whole photo including the background, who they are with, and any captions that have been added.

Special note: Be aware though that people can build fake profiles so if anything seems odd to you, go with your gut and try to get more information about anything that concerns you.

Sex Offender Records

The Dru Sjodin National Sex Offender Public Website (NSOPW.gov) allows you to search real-time registration information about sex offenders. You can search by name, state, county, city, or zip code for information on sex offender records.

Background Checks

There are companies that sell full background reports for a fee. You can search "Background check" online and many reporting sites will pop up for you to choose from.

Date Rape Drugs

As disappointing and uncomfortable this is to think about, this is information you must know to stay empowered. There are several date rape drugs and they are all relatively easy for someone to get a hold of. They can be crushed into a powder or can be purchased as a powder, spray, or liquid and then added to your drink or food. Most of these drugs are odorless, tasteless, and colorless leaving no way for you to detect them.

The best way to protect yourself is to know the warning signs and act quickly to safely remove yourself and/or others from the environment if you feel you or someone you are with has been drugged or that someone may be trying to drug you.

Warning Signs

If you ever feel dizzy, confused, overly sleepy, have trouble breathing, or seeing straight, after a drink or even just a few sips of something, someone may have "spiked" your drink/food with a date rape drug. Act quickly! Get a friend to leave with you right away, call a friend or family member to come get you, or call Uber, Lyft, or a taxi as a last resort. Make sure the driver knows where to find you. Tell whoever picks you up to take you to a hospital emergency room since you will not know what you ingested or how much. Since unknowingly mixing these drugs with alcohol can also make the effects worse, get medical attention as soon as possible.

Most date rape drugs have an amnesic effect, which means that you may not remember anything for hours after you have swallowed it. The awful people that do this type of thing can put the drug in your drink or food when you aren't looking or when you leave your drink/food unattended (like when you take a trip to the bathroom or the dance floor).

Special Note: You may think that you would never be around anyone that would do this type of thing to a woman. Unfortunately, there are too many people out there that do. I hate writing this section and I do not want you to feel you cannot go out and have fun. On the contrary, I want you to go out, have fun, and just have this information in the back of your mind so that if you ever need it for yourself or others, you will be empowered to better handle the situation.

Common Date Rape Drugs:

Here are a few drugs that have gotten reputations for being date rape drugs in the U.S. and worldwide. Once ingested they can start to take effect in as little as 20 minutes and can last up to 12 hours.

- *Rophynol:* Was actually the first to be called The Date Rape Drug and has many nicknames like: Roofies, Roopies, Roaches, Circles, and Mexican Valium. It is a type of benzodiazepine, an extremely strong tranquilizer that when taken can make it impossible for you to fight back.

- *Ecstasy:* Also known as Easy Lay, Goop, Liquid Ecstasy, Liquid X, Scoop, and "the love pill". It comes in a pill or liquid form and can cause psychological problems such as depression, confusion, severe anxiety and paranoia and can produce long-term, permanent physical problems like kidney, liver and brain damage.

- *Ambien® (generic drug name is Zolpidem):* A prescription sleep aid used by many people in the U.S. has also been commonly used as a date rape drug because it has a very strong amnesic effect. It comes in a pill, liquid, or even spray form. It is very dangerous to take without a doctor's supervision and can create hallucinations and strange behaviors (that are not remembered later) in people when under the influence of this drug.

If You Suspect You Have Been a Victim

If you ever suspect you have been a victim
of a drugging and/or date rape, immediately
collect as much evidence as you can to be
used in an investigation.

Save some of your urine in a clean,
sealable container, swab your mouth and private
area with cotton swabs, pull out a few strands
of your hair and store everything tightly sealed
in a refrigerator or freezer. Keep your panties
and any clothing with stains on them and pick
up any used condoms, seal them and put them
in the refrigerator too. Also, take pictures of the
scene both inside and outside and be sure to
get the address. Get yourself and the
evidence to a hospital as soon as possible
so they can run forensic tests.

Time is critical since the drug can be cleared from
your system very quickly once you are awake.
To locate a hospital or medical center that can
conduct the sexual assault forensic exams
and screen the evidence:

Contact the National Sexual Assault Hotline
800-656-HOPE
(Save this number into your phone)

Home

As a single woman, you will be meeting new people and making new relationships. Whether it is new friends or romantic partners, consider who you give your address to and/or allow in your home. While you are getting to know them consider meeting them at places instead of them picking you up and dropping you off at home. Once you have gotten to know them a little bit and you feel you can trust them, you can choose to give them your address information.

Special note: If you have children this is especially important since they also must feel safe where they live; they may not if they know you are allowing strangers to come into your home.

Your home is a special place. Even if it is not where you want to be forever, you should feel safe and comfortable in your living environment. This has to be a priority. If for any reason you (or your family) do not feel safe you must take steps to correct that.

Some ways you can improve your feelings of safety are:

- Install an alarm system
- Change the locks
- Add locks on doors and windows
- Lock gates
- Get a dog
- Get a roommate
- Plant thorny things around windows

- Move. It may seem like a hassle but the benefit of feeling safe and comfortable will be well worth your time and effort.

Emergency Water

If you are living on your own, or the sole adult with children, it is also important to understand how to prepare your living environment in case of a fire or an emergency.

Always have water bottles stored somewhere and rotate them out with new ones at least twice per year. People cannot survive long without water. Estimates show that although we can survive several weeks without food, we can only go without water for about 3-7 days depending on the conditions. Experts agree that you should keep at least 1 gallon per person, per day and that you should store at least a 3-day supply. (Don't forget your pets as they will need water also).

Fire Protection

Landlords are specifically required to check smoke and carbon monoxide alarms to ensure they work properly when a new tenant moves in. If you own your own place, you are the landlord and must do this regularly too.

Install smoke detectors and CO2 alarms.

Smoke alarms should be installed (or placed up high on a shelf, etc.) inside each bedroom, outside each sleeping area, outside the kitchen, and on every level of the home, including the basement, even if the level has no bedrooms.

CO2 detectors should also be on every floor and near every sleeping area but CO2 alarms should be installed/or be placed only about five feet from the ground to get the best protection since carbon monoxide mixes with the air (instead of rising like smoke does).

Since carbon monoxide is invisible and odorless, the alarm from a CO2 detector is the only way to know if you are being exposed to CO2.

Special Note: For both smoke detectors and CO detectors, if they are battery operated, it is a good habit to change all batteries every 6 months.

Fire Extinguishers

Fire extinguishers are also recommended to have on each floor of your house. Store them in the kitchen or near any source of heat or flame like fireplaces or gas appliances. You also want them in the bedrooms or bedroom closets so you can use them to put out small fires and/or create an escape route if needed for you and your family by spraying the solution on the fire to suppress the flames while you run out. There are three types of fires but you can get an extinguisher that works for all types so you do not have to wonder about what to do in a crisis. Get one where the label shows all three: A, B, and C fire types.

- **A** is ordinary combustibles (wood, paper, cloth)
- **B** is flammable liquids (gasoline, cooking oil, etc.)
- **C** is live electricity.

Fire Extinguishers do not last forever. They should be replaced and/or refilled about every 5 to 15 years or whenever they have been used (even if not completely emptied), or when the pressure gauge at the top of the canister has moved out of the green area and into the red area which can happen over time.

The recommended fire extinguisher sizes depend on what you will be able to move and lift during an emergency:

- A 5 lb. rechargeable one with a hose may be a good option for the rooms in your home.

- A 2 lb. disposable model may be a good option for your car.

The acronym PASS can help you remember how to use your fire extinguishers (but make sure to read the label on your extinguisher for more details):

- **P**ull the extinguisher's safety pin.

- **A**im the chemical at the <u>source</u> of the flames (not the flames themselves).

- **S**queeze the trigger and hold it, keep the extinguisher upright while you move the hose around at the different angles to spray.

- **S**weep the spray back and forth <u>at the source of the flames</u> (not the top of the flames) until the extinguisher runs dry or until you are out in a safe place.

Buying A Car

The first time I had to buy a car all on my own, I knew that my lack of knowledge would undoubtedly affect my final deal and I was very frustrated. The little girl in me desperately wanted some man to turn to for help but I knew I had to push through it on my own. It was such a stressful situation that, I decided to include this information here to empower you as you go through the process of buying your next car (new or used).

Researching a Car

Knowledge is power so the first thing you must do is spend time researching the type of car you want to buy. You want to evaluate car makes and models to narrow the list of the car(s) you are interested in, learn the value of a used car model(s), and/or the pricing set for the new model(s). Also, check the features that are available so that you know what you want included.

Some of the best sites to check are:

- **AutoTrader.com:** This is a great site for researching cars (new or used). It allows you to compare cars with lots of search selection criteria (body type, mileage, price, brand, safety, etc.) You can also post and sell your car on Autotrader.com

- **Kbb.com:** Kelley Blue Book has been around since the 1920s and is a great site which provides resources to help you research, price and shop for your car (new or used).

- **Consumerreports.org:** Consumer Reports has provided ratings and feedback on products to consumers for over 80 years. They have professional reviews but they require you to subscribe for a fee in order to access the information.

- **Dealers:** If you already know the car you want then visit the manufacturer's website (Example: Toyota.com) for information on your selected model.

A strategy that helped me to identify cars to consider was to search for top 10 lists. I did this to identify top new models and also used models from previous years.

Searching the top ten list of a previous year (for example: Top 10 SUV in 2016) gives you a list to start from as well as initial reviews and features in that year's models. If you are considering an older model you will want to look for the features available in the year the car model was made, not the features listed on the car dealer's website today with the current model.

Since a used car will not have a published standard invoice price, you will also want to research the recent resale prices for the specific car model you want to buy. You can find this information on several of the website suggestions in the bulleted list above.

If you are shopping for a new car, look for both the "invoice" price and the MSRP (manufacturer's suggested retail price). The "invoice" price shows what the dealer paid for the car. The MSRP is the price the manufacturer suggested for the car dealer to sell the car to make a profit. (Dealers frequently discount cars lower than

MSRP though so always try to pay less than the posted price.)

If you are planning to trade in your current car, also research the current resale value for that vehicle so you know what it is worth on the market. Having this information will help you negotiate your best trade in deal amount. Ensure that you research the price for a car as identical to your car as possible – with the same features, same model, and same year. For example: If your car is a sports model vs. a standard or luxury upgrade model, or if your car has GPS and seat warmers and was made in 2015 make sure to get comparison pricing for a car with those features.

Pre-financing Options

Many people walk into a car dealership, shop for a car and then get financed by the dealer all on the same day. However, you can often get better interest rates from banks, credit unions or even auto club type companies like AAA or USAA and they will pre-approve you for a set amount. Having your loan approved and walking into the dealership with your loan in hand can speed up your purchase process and make the experience less stressful and more enjoyable overall since you will not have to worry about approvals or interest rates, or spend hours with the finance department.

To get pre-approved for a car loan, check with any financial institutions you already do business with since you may be eligible for member rates or discounts, but feel free to explore other options too since there may be better deals out there with other providers.

Evaluating the Car

Whether you are shopping for a new or used car, always test drive the car before you buy it. Make sure the route you drive includes as much variety as possible. You will want to see how the car performs in different situations, like freeway driving, street driving, hills, and bumps.

Some things to evaluate during the test drive:

- How comfortable are you driving the car? Does the seat adjust to fit you well? Can you see well out of all the windows and mirrors?

- Does the dashboard provide all the info and tools you need? Can you see the items on the dashboard well? Do you understand the symbols and menus available?

- Are your guest passengers (or children) comfortable in the car? Do the back seats adjust well and get enough air from the vents? Sit in each of the seats and move them around to test them out.

- Test the windows, trunk, and all the electronics including the lights, seat warmers, outlets, and stereo to ensure they are all working properly (especially in used cars).

Inspection

Car dealerships will have already performed a multi-point inspection on all the used cars they sell and will have the results available for you to review. If you're planning to buy a used car from a person instead of a dealership though, it is important to have the car inspected by a mechanic before you finalize the deal.

Most sellers will allow you to have the car inspected, especially if you set up an inspection to be performed wherever the seller has the car. There are many mobile car inspection companies that provide these services. An online search for a "pre-purchase mobile car inspection" showed two national companies. I have included them here with their website blurb:

- **Lemonsquad.com**
  Company description: The leader in Nationwide Pre-Purchase Used Car Inspections. We inspect every car in every state across the USA- even Alaska and Hawaii.

- **Carchex.com**
  Company description: Carchex offers a qualified 155-point pre-purchase car inspection service for any car in the USA.

Most auto service locations: chain repair stores, dealership service departments, and independent garages also offer used car pre-purchase inspections if the car can be dropped off.

The inspection report will enable you to make fact based decisions about buying the car and will also provide key points of information that when shared with the seller, can help you negotiate the best deal.

Insurance Costs

Since you cannot legally drive a car in the U.S. without car insurance, check with your insurance company about any changes to your premium with the car you want to purchase. Once you have the new quote, you can calculate this cost into your car expense budget. You may want to check with other insurance companies also to evaluate your best options.

Special note: Car insurance premiums vary with the type of car covered. Several factors may increase insurance premiums. For example, sports cars have premiums higher than conventional cars due to safety concerns, or some cars have higher premiums because they are more frequently stolen. There are some standard discounts applied by most carriers, such as: good driver discounts, good student discounts, make sure you ask about what discounts are available to see if you qualify.

Your state car registration fee can also be different for each car. Check with your DMV prior to purchase so you can include this annual fee in your calculations.

Your Trade-In

If you have a trade-in it is a powerful piece of leverage in your negotiations. Do not mention it until the end of your buying process. If the dealer knows you will be trading in your car while you are negotiating the purchase price, he will not discount the car as much since he knows the trade-in credit will bring the price down further. Get the best deal for the car you want to buy first and then ask them what they will give you for your trade-in.

The Payments

Never negotiate a car price based on the monthly payment. This is a tough one for me because I tend to focus on my monthly budget and keeping my payments low. That is not the best strategy though since the dealer may offer you very attractive monthly payment amounts and then work the loan terms to generate maximum profit for the dealership and/or hide fees and interest totals in all of the paperwork (another reason to get pre-approved).

That said, make sure when you negotiate the purchase of the car you want, that you get the "full" purchase price from the seller before agreeing to anything or signing any documents. There can be many hidden costs which may raise the total amount you need to complete the deal.

Signing the Papers

Once everything is agreed, and they bring you the contract to sign, double check it for accuracy. To protect yourself and the legitimacy of the contract, make sure every section is complete. Do NOT sign any forms with any spaces left blank.

If you are trading in your current car, make sure the documents include the trade price you agreed to and that the amount has been credited toward your purchase. If the dealer is paying off any remaining loan or associated interest on your old car ensure it will be paid off right away and that you have all the details in writing.

Never drive off in your new car until the financing has been fully completed and any additional features or parts you negotiated in the deal are provided or installed in/on the car. Once you drive away in the car, the deal can be considered complete and there will be far less incentive for the dealer to complete the remaining job(s) for you in a timely manner.

Your Estate

Thinking about death is never fun but it is a necessary topic here to empower you and ensure that everything you work for, fight for, save, and build during your lifetime is also distributed the way you want it to be once you are gone. Your estate is everything that you own – all monies and all properties. Ensure that the people (or organizations) you love receive everything you have for them and those that you don't, have no way to take any of it. This is a vital piece in how your legacy plays out.

Remember your estate total can be reduced by any debt you have at the time of your death since it must be repaid and that the government can tax your estate heavily further reducing the values you plan to leave behind. All of this makes it extremely important that you organize everything, no matter how large or small, and protect it so your wishes are carried out when you are gone.

A will is not enough. It can spell out who you want to receive certain items but it will not protect anything from government taxes or from someone else staking claim to your possessions or assets. The way to protect your legacy and everything in your estate is by creating a Living Trust.

Living Trust

A living trust is a legal document that allows you to plan and provide detailed instructions on what will happen to your assets after you are gone. These instructions will be carried out, after your death by your successor trustee, a person or entity pre-determined by you and identified in your documents.

Special note: Your pre-determined successor trustee can be your spouse or other family member, a trusted friend, mentor, or an appointed lawyer, or law firm. You can also appoint co-trustees to work as a team to distribute your estate as planned.

Some of the many reasons to create your living trust:

- It remains a private document between the parties involved, and does not become part of the public record.

- It maintains power and control of your legacy because it ensures that your documented instructions will be followed after your death.

- It simplifies any financial obligations or questions, your beneficiaries would need to address reducing their stress while they deal with their loss.

- It avoids the probate process in court entirely, which saves time, money, frustration, and allows for a speedy distribution of your assets according to your written instructions.

- It reduces estate and gift taxes which would be imposed by the government during probate on your beneficiaries (any person or organizations that will be receiving assets from you).

- It gives you peace of mind that your family and other beneficiaries will be provided for.

Your living trust will be one of the most important documents you ever create. You can work directly with a lawyer, or you can find living trust forms online. If you want to complete the documents on your own, check Legalzoom.com or similar sites for tips and to purchase the proper forms.

Special note: If your company provides a Legal Plan as part of your employee benefits, you may be able to have an in-network lawyer create and execute the living trust documents at no additional costs since this is likely included in the plan. Check your benefits and plan details.

Whether you work with an attorney or not, you will still need to complete the following steps:

Make a list of all your assets.

Include everything of value you own on the list. Assets may include: your house and other real estate, cars, jewelry, art, collectibles, family heirlooms, and account information for checking, savings, retirement, 401K, stocks, bonds, and life insurance policies, etc. Include the account numbers and where/with what company these accounts are held.

Special note: If you have a safe deposit box include information on the bank address, the contents and the location of the key. Check with the bank about what happens to the box ownership when you die. To avoid restrictions, you may want to add a co-owner or executer to it now to ensure easy access to the contents for your estate distribution to be executed as planned.

Having this list for reference will show you the big picture and will be a tremendous help as you decide how, when, and to whom you would like your assets distributed once you are gone. This list will also be included in the trust package documents so the Trustees know what is included in your estate and how to find it.

Find the paperwork for your assets.

Now that you have a complete list, you will need to locate the paperwork showing ownership of your assets. Things like: the titles and deeds of property, stock certificates and life insurance policies, account numbers and statements. Having all of these details available will enable you and/or your attorney to get the details correctly documented in the trust to ensure your successor can locate and access the assets for proper distribution.

Determine the who, what, and when.

Within the trust you will name your beneficiaries, what you want to distribute to them, and when they will receive it. Beneficiaries (those whom will receive assets upon your death) can include family, friends or organizations (including charities). As part of your plan, you may also want to consider those people you do not want to receive anything and make sure to include those wishes in the written documents.

Since the trust allows you to spell out as much detail as desired, you can even set milestones or conditions for asset distribution. This means you can distribute portions of assets to multiple people, portions of assets at different times to people, or set up milestones for people to achieve rewards from the trust. The trust allows you to distribute assets any way you want to. One simple way is to set a certain age for children to inherit wealth but you can also include special payments for when they get married, graduate school, buy a home, start a business, or accomplish a goal. In addition, you can also specify annual amounts to be given to people or organizations.

You can be creative with how you set up the distribution plans. Speak with your lawyer if you have questions.

Choose a successor trustee

With a living trust, your named successor trustee will be the person that takes over to pay your debts and distribute your assets after your death or if you are seriously ill/injured and cannot voice your instructions. This should be someone you trust to follow your wishes and someone with good financial knowledge and behaviors.

Choose a guardian for your minor children.

If you have minor child(ren) you can name someone to take care of them and to manage their inheritance until they reach the age to manage it on their own. This language needs to be included in the trust package on the "pour-over-will" section detailing your instructions for your minor children.

Guardianship is such an incredibly important responsibility so discuss your plans with the person(s) you choose to be the guardian to be sure he/she is willing and able to accept the role in your absence.

Prepare the trust document.

Use the information you have gathered and decisions you have made to complete the trust documents.
You should then sign it in front of a notary.

Special note: All states do not require an official notary but it will strengthen the authenticity of your signature and avoid any issues after your death (especially if you prepared the documents yourself).

Share the trust document.

Once complete, make sure the successor trustee gets a copy of your full trust packet. Store your copy in a safe place, and tell people you trust where they can find it.

Special note: If you include a Medical Power of Attorney section in your trust packet (see section below), also provide a copy of everything to that person as your medical representative.

Transfer assets to fund the trust.

The transfer process is a critical step in setting up your trust. Once each piece is officially assigned to the Trust it becomes part of your official estate.

The way we assign each item to the trust can be different for different types of assets. For example, real estate deeds and titles must be changed to the name of the trust, bank accounts and investment accounts must name the trust as the sole beneficiary to the accounts.

This means that you no longer have a person as your beneficiary on your accounts or other assets; not your kids or your parents, relatives or friends, you must name your Trust as the beneficiary on each instead.

By naming your Trust the beneficiary, when you die all of your assets will be brought together and will then be distributed based on the instructions in your trust.

If you have an asset or assets that you do not name the Trust as the beneficiary, those assets will likely be outside of the Trust (file cabinet) and will go through probate, be taxed, and subjected to a judge's decision on distribution, instead of the instructions you detailed in your Trust.

Even if you have listed the asset in your trust documents, if you have not named the trust as the beneficiary for the asset, it may not be included in your Trust. Since your "people beneficiaries" will be designated by you in the trust document itself, your heirs will be taken care of according to your specific documented wishes in the trust papers.

Keep your living trust up to date.

Life constantly changes so you will need to review and update your trust each year. Some years you will have more changes than others. Some reasons why you may want to change your trust instructions are: births, deaths, marriages, divorces, investments, and property acquisitions and/or sales.

Since your list of assets in the trust can be in its own section, it is easy to add, delete, and change the information. Whenever you make any updates to any part of your trust package, alert your successor trustee and the guardian or medical power of attorney designee. Send an updated copy to them so they have a current copy for their files.

Medical Power of Attorney

This is an additional legal document that authorizes someone you pre-select to make medical decisions for you if you cannot do so due to illness or injury. The document includes information on your medical preferences and the medical power of attorney enables your designated representative to direct the treatment decisions for you until you get well enough to make your own decisions.

Special note: Consider that whenever someone steps into this role that it will be a stressful and highly emotional time for them. The person you designate should ideally handle stress well and be able to question and understand the medical situation. They should be willing and able to fulfill your wishes as needed based on the instructions you have expressed in the document.

Facebook Legacy Contact

If you want to make sure that that your friends and family are notified in the event of your death, a simple step you can implement is to establish a Legacy Contact on your Facebook account. Since most adults now have Facebook accounts, it is a quick way to share information. Your Facebook account will already be linked to your contacts so when a post is sent out from your Facebook account it will reach your community very quickly.

Facebook provides the option to assign a legacy contact to each account. At the time of your death, your pre-assigned legacy contact will be given access to your account.

To set this up, go to your Account Settings in your Facebook account. Then in the menu click on Legacy Contact. Click on the person you select for this role. (You can only select someone who is one of your Facebook friends).

Once selected, they will receive an automatic email message from Facebook saying you have designated them your legacy contact. Let them know if you have specific wishes for what/when you would like them to post in the event of your death. If desired you can even add these notes to your Living Trust documents.

Be Thoughtful.

_____

_____

_____

_____

_____

_____

_____

_____

_____

_____

_____

Be Thoughtful.

_____

_____

_____

_____

_____

_____

_____

_____

_____

_____

_____

"Everything is hard before it is easy." ~Goethe	"If you are always trying to be normal you will never know how amazing you can be." ~Maya Angelou	"Today you are you, that is truer than true. There is no one alive who is youer than you." ~Dr. Seuss
"Be a voice, not an echo." ~Unknown	"If you think you are too small to make a difference, try sleeping with a mosquito." ~Dalai Lama	"Your beliefs don't make you a better person, your behavior does." ~Sukhrai S. Dhillon
"You wouldn't worry so much about what other's think of you if you realized how seldom they do." ~Eleanor Roosevelt	"You have to be unique, and different, and shine in your own way." ~Lady Gaga	"Life is like a box of chocolates, you never know what you're gonna get." ~Forrest Gump
"Be who you are and say what you feel because those who mind don't matter and those who matter don't mind." ~Dr. Seuss	"Being a little weird is just a natural side-effect of being awesome" ~ Sue Fitzmaurice	"Life is not about finding yourself, it is about creating yourself." ~Unknown

RESOURCES

Introduction

Intro: Scientists Finally Figure Out How Bees Fly
By Sara Goudarzi (January 9, 2006)
https://www.livescience.com/528-scientists-finally-figure-bees-fly.html

Intro: Single Mother Statistics
By Dawn Lee (Updated September 29, 2017)
https://singlemotherguide.com/single-mother-statistics/

Intro: America's Families and Living Arrangements: 2016, Table A1 Release Number: CB17-TPS.62
By United States Census Bureau (August 14, 2017, Revised August 16, 2017)
https://www.census.gov/newsroom/facts-for-features/2017/single-americans-week.html

Intro: Women Travel Statistics and Women Travel Trends
By Marybeth Bond (March 2017)
https://gutsytraveler.com/women-travel-statistics-women-travel-trends/

Happy

Happy – Mind-Body Connection: - Bob Dunham is founder of the Institute for Generative Leadership (IGL). (Not dated)
http://generateleadership.com/courses/glp/glp-faculty-staff-guests/

Happy – Mind-Body Connection: Mind-Body Connection - Understanding the Psycho-Emotional Roots of Disease
By Jennifer Weinberg (not dated)
https://chopra.com/articles/mind-body-connection-understanding-the-psycho-emotional-roots-of-disease

Happy – Mind-Body Connection: Emotions & Health
By National Institutes of Health Emotions and Health (Winter 2008)
https://medlineplus.gov/magazine/issues/winter08/articles/winter08pg4.html

Happy – Happy Chemicals: Hacking Into Your Happy Chemicals: Dopamine, Serotonin, Endorphins and Oxytocin THE BLOG
By Thai Nguyen (updated Dec 20, 2014)
http://www.huffingtonpost.com/thai-nguyen/hacking-into-your-happy-c_b_6007660.html

Happy – Happy Chemicals: How to Boost Serotonin
By WikiHow.com (not dated)
https://www.wikihow.com/Boost-Serotonin

Happy – Happy Chemicals: How to Increase Dopamine Naturally

By Deane Alban (not dated)
https://bebrainfit.com/increase-dopamine/

Happy – Happy Chemicals: Spark: The Revolutionary
New Science of Exercise and the Brain
By Dr. John Ratey (copyright 2008)
Spark: The Revolutionary New Science of Exercise and
the Brain

Happy – Happy Chemicals: Habits of a Happy Brain:
Retrain Your Brain to Boost Your Serotonin, Dopamine,
Oxytocin, & Endorphin Levels
By Dr. Loretta Graziano Breuning (copyright 2016)
https://www.amazon.com/Habits-Happy-Brain-
Serotonin-Endorphin-ebook/dp/B0178M3LNA

Happy – Action: Action - Five Powerful Reasons to
Take Action Today
By Henrik Edberg (May 13, 2009)
https://www.positivityblog.com/five-powerful-reasons-
to-take-action-today/

Happy – Action: The 5 Second Rule: Transform your
Life, Work, and Confidence with Everyday Courage
By Mel Robbins (copyright 2017)
https://melrobbins.com/5-second-rule/

Happy – Mindsets: 31 Benefits of Gratitude You Didn't
Know About: How Gratitude Can Change Your Life
By H H (not dated)
 http://happierhuman.com/benefits-of-gratitude/
Happy - Support: Credential Abbreviations
By NetworkTherapy.com (not dated)
https://www.networktherapy.com/directory/credentials.asp

Happy - Support: About ICF
By The International Coach Federation (ICF) (not dated)
https://coachfederation.org/about

Happy - Nature: How Nature is good for our health and happiness
By Jeremy Coles (April 20, 2016)
http://www.bbc.com/earth/story/20160420-how-nature-is-good-for-our-health-and-happiness

Happy - Nature: 30 Days Wild: Development and Evaluation of a Large-Scale Nature Engagement Campaign to Improve Well-Being
By Miles Richardson, Adam Cormack, Lucy McRobert, Ralph Underhill PLOS (published February 18, 2016)
https://doi.org/10.1371/journal.pone.0149777

Happy - Nature: Immerse Yourself in a Forest for Better Health
By Department of Environmental Conservation (not dated)
http://www.dec.ny.gov/lands/90720.html

Happy - Nature: 5 Benefits of Being Outdoors
By Jill L. Ferguson (not dated)
https://www.huffingtonpost.com/entry/5-benefits-of-being-outdoors_us_5938266ce4b014ae8c69dce0

Happy - Nature: How Does Nature Impact Our Wellbeing? By the University of Minnesota's Earl E. Bakken Center for Spirituality & Healing (not dated)
https://www.takingcharge.csh.umn.edu/enhance-your-wellbeing/environment/nature-and-us/how-does-nature-impact-our-wellbeing

Happy - Career: 14 Companies That Can Help Re-Entry Moms Get Their Careers Back
By Maricar Santos (October 18, 2016)
https://www.workingmother.com/on-ramping-programs-for-working-moms

Happy - Career: Resume tips for full-time parents returning to work
By Kim Isaacs, Monster resume expert (not dated)
https://www.monster.com/career-advice/article/resume-tips-parents-returning-to-work

Happy - Career: How to Write the Perfect Resume for Your Job Hunt
By Alison Doyle (updated July 02, 2017)
https://www.thebalance.com/job-resumes-4073657

Happy - Career: Interview Tips for Stay-at-Home Moms Reentering Today's Job Market
By Sharon Reed Abboud (not dated)
https://www.monster.com/career-advice/article/All-Moms-Work-Confidence-Interview

Happy - Career: 6 questions to ask an employer during an interview
By Joe Turner (not dated)
https://www.monster.com/career-advice/article/Six-Must-Ask-Interview-Questions

Happy - Wealth: Suze Orman (suzeorman.com)

Happy - Wealth: Daily Worth (dailyworth.com)

Happy - Wealth: Women's Institute For a Secure Retirement website (wiserwomen.org)

Happy - Wealth: Guide to Financial Independence for Women (thesimpledollar.com)
https://www.thesimpledollar.com/guide-to-financial-independence-for-women/

Health / Beauty

Health/Beauty – Sleep: The Effects of Sleep Deprivation on Your Body
By Ann Pietrangelo, Stephanie Watson, reviewed by Dr. Deborah Weatherspoon, PhD, RN, CRNA (June 5, 2017)
https://www.healthline.com/health/sleep-deprivation/effects-on-body

Health/Beauty – Sleep: Why lack of sleep is bad for your health
By NHS Choices (last reviewed: June 15, 2015)
https://www.nhs.uk/Livewell/tiredness-and-fatigue/Pages/lack-of-sleep-health-risks.aspx

Health/Beauty – Vitamins: Top Vitamins and Minerals for Natural Stress Relief
By <u>Deane Alban</u> (not dated)
<u>https://bebrainfit.com/vitamins-minerals-stress-relief/</u>

Health/Beauty – Vitamins: 10 Nutrients Scientifically Proven to Make You Feel Awesome
By Maya Dangerfield (December 31, 2013)
<u>https://greatist.com/happiness/nutrients-boost-mood</u>

Health/Beauty – Vitamins: 12 Patient-Approved Natural Supplements for Depression
By <u>Therese Borchard</u> (not dated)
<u>https://www.everydayhealth.com/columns/therese-borchard-sanity-break/patient-approved-natural-supplements-depression/</u>

Health/Beauty – Vitamins: Benefits of B Complex Vitamins
By Cathy Wong, ND | Reviewed by Richard N. Fogoros, MD (Updated June 10, 2018)
<u>https://www.verywellfit.com/b-complex-vitamins-89411</u>

Health/Beauty – Vitamins: Why Is Vitamin B Complex Important, and Where Do I Get It?
By Emily Cronkleton Medically reviewed by Natalie Olsen, RD, LD, ACSM EP-C (April 2, 2018)
<u>https://www.healthline.com/health/food-nutrition/vitamin-b-complex</u>

Health/Beauty – Vitamins: Vitamin D Deficiency
WebMD Medical Reference (Reviewed by Christine
Mikstas, RD, LD on May 16, 2018)
https://www.webmd.com/diet/guide/vitamin-d-deficiency#1

Health/Beauty – Vitamins: Symptoms & Diseases
Associated With Vitamin D Deficiency
By Dr. Frank Lipman (September 15, 2009)
https://www.bewell.com/blog/symptoms-diseases-associated-with-vitamin-d-deficiency/

Health/Beauty – Vitamins: 8 Ways Magnesium
Relieves Anxiety and Stress
By Deane Alban (not dated)
https://bebrainfit.com/magnesium-anxiety-stress/

Health/Beauty – Vitamins: What Is a Magnesium
Test?
By WebMD (not dated)
https://www.webmd.com/a-to-z-guides/magnesium-test#1

Health/Beauty – Vitamins: 7 Unusual Signs of Iron
Deficiency. Hair loss, fatigue, and a swollen tongue can
all be symptoms of low iron levels.
By Ashley Welch (not dated)
https://www.everydayhealth.com/news/unusual-signs-iron-deficiency/

Health/Beauty – Vitamins: The Facts on Omega-3 Fatty Acids
By WebMD (not dated)
https://www.webmd.com/healthy-aging/omega-3-fatty-acids-fact-sheet#1

Health/Beauty – Vitamins: 10 Powerful Zinc Benefits, Including Fighting Cancer
By Dr. Axe (not dated)
https://draxe.com/zinc-benefits/

Health/Beauty – Vitamins: Probiotics Benefits, Foods and Supplements
By Dr. Axe (not dated)
https://draxe.com/probiotics-benefits-foods-supplements/

Health/Beauty – Body Therapies: Pranic Healing
By Wikipedia, the free encyclopedia (not dated)
https://en.wikipedia.org/wiki/Pranic_healing

Health/Beauty – Body Therapies: Reiki - 7 health benefits of Reiki that will boggle your mind
By Mita Majumdar (September 25, 2014)
http://www.thehealthsite.com/diseases-conditions/health-benefits-of-reiki/

Health/Beauty - Skin care: 17 Home Remedies For Wrinkles
By The Editors of Prevention (June 22, 2014)
https://www.prevention.com/health/17-home-remedies-for-wrinkles

Health/Beauty - Skin care: 6 Everyday Habits That Are Giving You More Wrinkles
By Alexandra Duron (December 16, 2014)
https://www.prevention.com/beauty/habits-cause-wrinkles

Health/Beauty - Skin care: Ask Bella: I'm Confused About the Different Types of Exfoliants
By POPSUGAR Beauty AU (November 7, 2011)
https://www.popsugar.com.au/beauty/Different-Types-Exfoliants-20302849

Health/Beauty – Makeup: How To Buy And Apply The Right Foundation For Your Skin Type
By Bobbi Brown (September 14, 2015)
https://www.prevention.com/beauty/foundation-makeup-tips-bobbi-brown

Health/Beauty – Makeup: 10 Best Foundations For Every Age And Skin Type
By Katie Becker (May 24, 2017)
https://www.prevention.com/beauty/anti-aging-foundation

Health/Beauty – Makeup: The Best Foundations to Wear if You Have Sensitive Skin
By Erin Lukas (June 19, 2017)
http://www.instyle.com/beauty/makeup/best-foundations-for-sensitive-skin

Health/Beauty – Makeup: The Best Ingredients to Control Oily Skin By Amber Katz (not dated)
https://www.everydayhealth.com/beauty-pictures/the-best-ingredients-to-control-oily-skin.aspx

Health/Beauty – Makeup: 6 Anti-Aging Foundations That Erase Years Instantly
By Kristin Canning (February 01, 2017)
http://www.health.com/beauty/anti-aging-foundations

Health/Beauty – Makeup: 5 Makeup Tricks to Help You Look Younger
By Katie Dickens (July 14, 2017)
http://www.elle.com/beauty/makeup-skin-care/news/a14978/anti-aging-makeup-tips/

Health/Beauty – Makeup: Slideshow 10 Makeup & Beauty Tips for Older Women
By Variety Moms (not dated)
http://www.varietymoms.com/makeup-beauty-tips-women-oda/?utm_source=outbrain&utm_medium=referral&utm_term=Health.com+%28Time+Inc.%29&utm_content=Health.com&utm_campaign=beauty-desktop-t1

Health/Beauty – Makeup: What Is Makeup Primer, and Do You Need It?
By Dana Oliver (12/21/2017)
https://www.huffingtonpost.com/entry/what-is-makeup-primer-do-you-need-it_us_5a3b390ae4b0b0e5a79f8680

Health/Beauty – Makeup: How to Choose the Best Makeup Primers for Your Skin Type
By Maya Adivi (updated on August 30, 2016)
http://www.fashionisers.com/beauty-tips/how-to-choose-best-makeup-primers/

Health/Beauty – Makeup: Makeup Tips for Older Women: 6 Simple Techniques You Can Use Today
By Margaret Manning (not dated)
http://sixtyandme.com/makeup-tips-for-older-women-simple-techniques-for-better-makeup-application/

Health/Beauty – Makeup: Eye Makeup For Older Women
By Tricia Cusden (not dated)
https://www.lookfabulousforever.com/blog/eye-makeup-for-older-women/

Health/Beauty - Cosmetic Surgery: This Is The Top Plastic Surgery Trend of 2017
By Jenna Rosenstein (December 14, 2017)
https://www.harpersbazaar.com/beauty/skin-care/a14436319/top-plastic-cosmetic-surgery-trends-2017/

Health/Beauty – Teeth whitening: The best teeth whitening products
By Reviews.com (October 9, 2017)
https://www.reviews.com/teeth-whitening-products/

Health/Beauty - Personal grooming: Intimate Grooming: What Women Need to Know
By Carol Sorgen (not dated)
https://www.webmd.com/beauty/features/female-intimate-grooming#2

Health/Beauty - Personal grooming: Turns Out 84 Percent Of Women Groom Their Pubic Hair
By Annie Tomlin (June 30, 2016)
https://www.self.com/story/turns-out-84-percent-of-women-groom-their-pubic-hair

Health/Beauty - Personal grooming: 40 Percent of Men Have Asked Their Partner to Change Their Pubic Hair, A Cosmopolitan.com survey reveals shocking disparities between men's and women's views of pubic hair.
By Amelia Thomson-DeVeaux (April 26, 2017)
http://www.cosmopolitan.com/sex-love/a9535211/pubic-hair-removal-trends-stats/

Health/Beauty – Fitness: Fitness Industry Analysis 2017 - Cost & Trends
By Matt Sena (not dated)
https://www.franchisehelp.com/industry-reports/fitness-industry-report/

Health/Beauty – Fitness: The Best Fitness Blogs of the Year
By Colleen de Bellefonds (April 28, 2017)
https://www.healthline.com/health/fitness-exercise/best-blogs-of-the-year#1

Safety

Safety - Home: Where to Place Smoke Detectors in Your Home Safety Equipment for Your Home
By Timothy Thiele (updated 07/24/17)
https://www.thespruce.com/where-to-place-smoke-detectors-1152485

Safety - Home: How to Install Carbon Monoxide Detectors in Your Home
By Danny Lipford (not dated)
https://www.todayshomeowner.com/video/how-to-install-carbon-monoxide-detectors-in-your-home/

Safety - Home: How to Choose and Use Fire Extinguishers
By John Kelsey of This Old House magazine (not dated)
https://www.thisoldhouse.com/ideas/how-to-choose-and-use-fire-extinguishers

Safety - Home: How Much Water Should You Store?
By Emergency Essentials (July 24, 2015)
https://beprepared.com/blog/18680/much-water-store/

Safety – Dating: The History of Online Dating From 1695 to Now
By Susie Lee (updated December 06, 2017)
https://www.huffingtonpost.com/susie-lee/timeline-online-dating-fr_b_9228040.html

Safety – Dating: Keep Yourself Safe Online With These 10 Tips on Using Social Networking
By Linda Lowen (updated February 07, 2016)
https://www.thoughtco.com/social-networking-safety-tips-for-women-3534076

Safety – Dating: 10 Social Networking Safety Tips - Social Media Safety Tips for Women, Girls
By Linda Lowen (updated March 12, 2017)
https://www.thoughtco.com/social-networking-safety-tips-for-women-3534076

Safety – Dating: How to do a free online background check
By The Kim Komando Show (published April 13, 2013)
http://www.foxnews.com/tech/2013/04/13/how-to-do-free-online-background-check.html

Safety – Dating: How to Do a Background Check on a Guy
By: Collene Lawhorn-Sanchez (not dated)
https://datingtips.match.com/background-check-guy-13443262.html

Safety – Dating: How to perform a background check before your online date
By Rachel Esco (Aug 31, 2015)
http://www.sheknows.com/love-and-sex/articles/1094441/how-to-perform-a-background-check-before-your-online-date

Safety – Dating: Dating Services - US Market Research Report
By IBIS World (December 2017)
https://www.ibisworld.com/industry-trends/market-research-reports/other-services-except-public-administration/personal-laundry/dating-services.html

Safety – Dating: Fact Tank - Our Lives in Numbers
5 facts about online dating
By Aaron Smith and Monica Anderson (February 29, 2016)
http://www.pewresearch.org/fact-tank/2016/02/29/5-facts-about-online-dating/

Safety – Dating: Online Dating Statistics
By Statistic Brain (not dated)
http://www.statisticbrain.com/online-dating-statistics/

Safety – Dating: The 23 Best Online Dating Sites in the United States
By Visa Hunter (not dated)
http://www.visahunter.com/articles/the-best-online-dating-sites-in-the-united-states/

Safety – Dating: 15 ways to make your online dating profile stand out
By Francesca Rice (August 31, 2017 5:11 pm)
http://www.marieclaire.co.uk/life/sex-and-relationships/15-ways-to-make-your-online-dating-profile-stand-out-from-the-pack-1-118673

Safety – Dating: How to Write a Good Online Dating Profile
By wikiHow (not dated)
https://www.wikihow.com/Write-a-Good-Online-Dating-Profile

Safety – Dating: How To Write a Dating Profile, Even If You're Not A Writer
By Colleen Healy (August 15, 2016)
https://www.zoosk.com/date-mix/online-dating-advice/online-dating-profile-tips/how-to-write-a-dating-profile/

Safety – Dating:13 Ways to Make Sure You Have the Best Profile Picture
By Cosette Jarrett (September 5, 2017)
https://www.zoosk.com/date-mix/online-dating-advice/online-dating-profile-tips/best-profile-picture/

Safety – Dating: Tinder Dating Tips: The Definitive Script For Picking Up Girls On Tinder
By Wingman (not dated)
http://get-a-wingman.com/tinder-dating-tips-the-definitive-script-for-picking-up-girls-on-tinder/

Safety – Dating: 11 tips for actually getting a date on Tinder, from their youngest female exec
By Dusty Baxter-Wright (Nov 20, 2016)
http://www.cosmopolitan.com/uk/love-sex/news/a41110/tinder-dating-tips/

Safety – Going Out: Types of Date Rape Drugs
By Samantha Gluck (not dated)
https://www.healthyplace.com/abuse/rape/date-rape-drugs-types-and-how-date-rape-drugs-work/

Safety – Going Out: Date Rape Drugs - Rohypnol
By Foundation for a Drug-Free World (not dated)
http://www.drugfreeworld.org/drugfacts/prescription/rohypnol.html

Safety – Going Out: Date Rape Drugs - What is Ecstasy?
By Foundation for a Drug-Free World (not dated)
http://www.drugfreeworld.org/drugfacts/ecstasy/what-is-ecstasy.html

Safety - Car buying: How to Buy a Car-15 Essential Tips to Get the Best Deal
By David Bakke (not dated)
https://www.moneycrashers.com/how-to-buy-car-tips/

Safety - Car buying: Do's and Don'ts When Buying a Car From a Dealer
By Consumer Reports (July 18, 2017)
https://www.consumerreports.org/buying-a-car/dos-and-donts-when-buying-a-car-from-a-dealer/

Safety - Car buying: Men vs. Women: The Gender Divide of Car Buying
By CJ Pony Parts (updated September 29, 2017)
https://www.cjponyparts.com/resources/men-vs-women-car-buying

Safety - Car buying: Inspect That Used Car Before Buying

By Edmunds (November 13th, 2013)

https://www.edmunds.com/car-buying/inspect-that-used-car-before-buying.html

Safety – Identity Protection: Identity Fraud Hits Record High with 15.4 Million U.S. Victims in 2016, Up 16 Percent According to New Javelin Strategy & Research Study

By Javelin Strategy & Research (@JavelinStrategy) (February 1, 2017)

https://www.javelinstrategy.com/press-release/identity-fraud-hits-record-high-154-million-us-victims-2016-16-percent-according-new

Safety – Identity Protection: What You Need to Know About Identity Theft Protection

By Brian O'Connell (Jun 26, 2017 12:22 PM EDT)

https://www.thestreet.com/story/14195200/1/what-you-need-to-know-about-identity-theft-protection.html#2

Safety – Identity Protection: Identity Protection - What Every Consumer Should Know

By Nick – Consumers Advocate.org   (May 20, 2014)

https://www.consumersadvocate.org/id-theft-protection/identity-protection

Safety – Identity Protection: Best Identity Theft Protection Services of 2018

By Carolyn Dorant (updated on August 14, 2017

https://www.thesimpledollar.com/best-identity-theft-protection-services/

Safety – Estate: Make a Living Trust: A Quick Checklist
By <u>Michelle Fabio, Esq.</u> (not dated)
<u>https://www.legalzoom.com/articles/make-a-living-trust-a-quick-checklist</u>

Safety – Estate: Top 5 Must Dos Before You Write a Living Trust
By <u>Michelle Fabio, Esq.</u> (not dated)
<u>https://www.legalzoom.com/articles/top-5-must-dos-before-you-write-a-living-trust</u>

Safety – Estate: Medical Power of Attorney: What Is a Medical Power of Attorney Form?
By Edward A. Haman, Esq. (not dated)
<u>https://www.legalzoom.com/articles/what-is-a-medical-power-of-attorney-form</u>

Be Thoughtful.

_____

_____

_____

_____

_____

_____

_____

_____

_____

_____

_____

Be Thoughtful.

_____

_____

_____

_____

_____

_____

_____

_____

_____

_____

——————

Be Thoughtful.

_____

_____

_____

_____

_____

_____

_____

_____

_____

_____

_____

I am grateful.

I feel truly grateful for being able to write and publish this book. I strongly wish from my heart that the information included here has helped to provide each woman that reads this book with strength, knowledge, power, and perspective to embrace new experiences and to build and live a life you enjoy in this new phase of your existence.

Please join us on our Facebook page:
Newlysinglewomencommunity

And our website:
Newlysinglewomencommunity.com

Live in possibility,
Joy Casillas
joy@newlysinglewomencommunity.com